BALLADS, SONGS AND SNATCHES

(A Play - with Music - in Four Acts)

Glenys Groves

2

A wandering minstrel I -

A thing of shreds and patches,

Of ballads, songs and snatches,

And dreamy lullaby!

NANKI-POO (The Mikado)

On the following pages there will be found what amounts to blatant 'name-dropping' - both people and places. For this I make no apologies whatsoever. I have been extremely fortunate over the course of my career to have had the privilege of working with luminaries of the entertainment world and at the most iconic of venues. As far as this book is concerned, to be modest about this would serve no purpose at all.

INDEX

PROLOGUE

ACT 1

FIRST INTERVAL

ACT 2

SECOND INTERVAL

ACT 3

(Continued on next page)

THIRD INTERVAL

ACT 4

PROLOGUE

Oh no! The panic rose in my throat and I swallowed hard. I felt my face flush and my heart began hammering, so loud I almost expected my immediate neighbour to glance over in curiosity. Nine and ten years old, we were all in the school hall, standing in neat rows, a yard apart, lustily singing the folk song 'Sweet Nightingale'. Mr Roberts, the Headmaster of Oak Farm Junior School, had decided to form a School Choir and was now embarking on the selection process. He worked his way methodically up and down the rows, pausing occasionally to listen to an individual piping voice, and then a gentle tap on the shoulder indicated a chosen candidate. I had just seen my very best friend, Janet Dudman, receive the required acknowledgement and Mr Roberts advanced towards me. "As She Sings In The Valley Belo-o-o-o-o-o-o-o-oh" Hooray! My favourite bit of the song. I cranked up the volume and my shoulder tensed in anticipation of the expected tap. Suddenly Mr Roberts paused, momentarily distracted by a pupil, perhaps fidgeting, in the back row. He strode purposefully towards the miscreant as we continued to warble the end of the chorus: "As She Sings In The Valley Below..."

Horrors! When he returned to the task in hand, he started back beside the person *behind* me. *He had missed me out*. I was devastated, although that had nothing to do with the singing. I had immediately realised that it meant Janet and I would not be sharing an activity: she would be going to choir practice and I would be excluded. We *always* did things together, and I knew she would be as unhappy about the situation as me. I was desperate, my throat constricted; no further sound could come out and tears began to well. What on earth was I to do? For the rest of the song my mind was racing: should (or could) I pretend that I *had* been chosen? Could (or should) I persuade Janet that she *hadn't* been chosen? I had to have a plan. Think, Glenys, think.

Eventually the song finished, and Mr Roberts gave brief instructions for the new choir members to present themselves at lunch break the following day. Although dismissed, I stood rooted to the spot; the sick feeling in my stomach prevented my legs from carrying me away from this awful place of hideous disappointment. Then, my mind made up, I slowly advanced towards Mr Roberts who was gathering papers up from the top of the grand piano. Eat your heart out, Oliver Twist.

"Please Sir..."

Mr Roberts turned and glanced at the stricken, and by now tear-stained, little face before him

"...I think you missed me out, by mistake."

He must surely have been quite bemused (and probably even amused), but I guess he considered a willing volunteer was worth two conscripts. He probably even saw Janet hovering anxiously at the doorway and put two and two together, but to my intense relief he replied: "Very well, you may join the choir, if you wish." IF I WISH???

Crisis over, Janet and I skipped down the school drive. We would be attending choir practices together.

Little did I realise that this act of kindness would prove to be a pivotal moment in my life.

ACT 1 - Scene 1

LITTLE ACORNS

The choir practices proved most enjoyable and the Oak Farm Junior School Choir thrived under Mr Roberts' enthusiastic leadership. Our first entry in the Uxbridge Music Festival (choir class, age 12 and under) was very successful and the following year Mr Roberts decided that all choir members should learn the set piece appropriate to their age and enter the solo singing class. I still remember my song; it was called 'My Mouse'.

"Don't be nervous - sing to the clock at the back of the Hall!" was the final encouragement at our last rehearsal. Advice totally wasted on me. As a result of a recent incident involving my bicycle and the kerb, I was now the very unhappy possessor of a pair of round, pink wire-framed National Health spectacles, and I was absolutely NOT wearing them to sing on stage. So on the day I could not even see the front row of chairs, let alone the clock at the back of the hall. In a total (but comfortable) blur, I started to tell the story of My Mouse. I can still recall singing that song. It was a totally amazing experience - I LOVED it! To my immense pleasure, the audience (and the Adjudicator) also enjoyed my rendition. I was hooked! Then and there, aged nine, I decided that I wanted to be a singer.

To this end, when it came to entering the sixth form for a two-year course as a stepping-stone to University, I opted instead for the one-year 'Commercial' course. I justified this decision to study shorthand and typing as a 'backstop', just in case my intended career in the theatre did not work out. A good decision, as it turned out.

However, back to music and dear Mavis. Mavis Bennett was a very well respected singing teacher, and deservedly so. An advocate of the *'Bel Canto'* Old School of voice production, under her expert tuition young voices were nurtured and older pupils were groomed to make their way into the music profession. She had herself been a very successful solo singer until a botched tonsillectomy just before the Second World War had badly damaged her vocal cords and totally robbed her of her singing voice. After the war she retrained as a voice teacher, and she was truly inspirational. Only now do I appreciate how it must have pained her not to be able to demonstrate sung notes and phrases. Mavis held regular soirées when her pupils would perform for each other, the older singers proving to be a great inspiration for the younger set. Such was her reputation as a teacher that the audience on these occasions would often include various luminaries from the professional world, on a low-key talent spotting exercise. It was through a couple of these soirées that I had an introduction to both Robert Keys (then Assistant Head of Music at the Royal Opera House) and John McCarthy who ran the world famous professional recording choir, the Ambrosian Singers. Both these gentlemen featured heavily in my professional career and I remained close to them for the rest of their lives.

The BBC had started to plan a series of operas to be filmed in the TV studio, directed by the distinguished television director Brian Large. John McCarthy was tasked to provide a chorus from his vast address book of 'session singers'.

John booked me and a couple of other Mavis' pupils for our first 'TV Opera': Tchaikovsky's *Eugene Onegin*. I was 17 years old, had just left school and was working as a shorthand typist for the Clerical and Medical Assurance Company in their branch office in Carey Street, London WC2. I negotiated the necessary 3 weeks off, and embarked on my 'first choice' chosen career.

Taking part in these operas were many well-known and established singers, and also many young soloists who would then go on to have great careers on the operatic stage. For example, *Eugene Onegin* (filmed in black and white, just before colour television was developed) showcased a young (Dame) Margaret Price, John Shirley-Quirk, and Robert Tear. *La Traviata*, which followed (in colour) featured Elizabeth Harewood, John Brecknock and Norman Bailey with Alan Opie, Philip Langridge and Michael Rippon in the small supporting roles. *The Count of Luxembourg* starred Adele Leigh and Nigel Douglas. The great Norman Bailey appeared as *The Flying Dutchman* and *Macbeth* - with up and coming Neil Shicoff as Macduff. It was a wonderful opportunity for a very young would-be singer to work with some truly great artists, and I managed to acquire a much-coveted Equity card as well.

One day, at my regular Saturday morning lesson Mavis said to me: "When I was your age I joined the D'Oyly Carte Opera Company - you should apply for an audition." This I duly did and a few weeks later, instead of driving me to Stoke Poges, my parents and I set off for The Savoy Theatre in the Strand, central London. The D'Oyly Carte Head Office was at 1 Savoy Hill, WC2, and Bridget D'Oyly Carte owned the prime piece of real estate that included The Savoy Hotel and Theatre. I presented myself at the stage door as arranged and for the first time in my life entered the hallowed world of backstage professional theatre. What a shock! Whilst the front of house is all glamorous plush, gilt, velvet and chandeliers, backstage is a maze of concrete floored corridors, naked light bulbs, cracked washbasins and overflowing waste bins. My eyes were on stalks as I made my way to the prompt corner at the side of the stage. But I had an audition to perform. I gave the copy of my music to the Stage Manager to convey to the accompanist in the orchestra pit and waited to be sent on to the stage. Soon I was told I could go on. Naturally, off came the glasses (those days were definitely pre-contact lenses) and I strode purposefully towards the centre of the stage. Somewhat dazzled by the bright stage lights and definitely hampered by the absence of corrective eyewear, I collided clumsily with a sofa that was part of the set for the current production. Picking myself up from the floor, I marched to the front of the stage and peered into the auditorium. On discerning some shapes in the right-hand front stalls, I fixed them with a beaming smile and launched into my audition aria 'Little Polly Flinders' by Michael Diack. Finishing with a flourishing cadenza and a ringing top B flat, I flashed them another smile and prepared to leave the stage. To my horror, a voice from way back on the *left* side of the auditorium called out: "Thank you Miss Groves - do tell us a little about yourself." I had been singing to a pile of coats in the front row! Fortunately the coats must have enjoyed my performance, as the following Wednesday I received a letter offering me a contract with the Company.

Mavis had always impressed upon me the importance of dressing well for an audition or performance: ("They might not remember what you sang, but they will always remember what you wore, my dear.") This advice came back to me several months later at a grand D'Oyly Carte reception, attended by no less a personage than Miss Bridget D'Oyly Carte herself. Nervously, I was ushered in her direction by Frederick Lloyd, the Company Manager. "Allow me to introduce to you our newest chorister, Glenys" he said. "Ah yes," she replied, looking me up and down, "the little girl in the charming brown dress." I will never know how much my audition success was down to brown and white Prince of Wales check and a white Peter Pan collar. (Oh, and of course the new red shoes!)

ACT 1 - Scene 2

A WANDERING MINSTREL

The D'Oyly Carte Opera Company was a touring company, performing for up to four weeks at a time at all the major theatres in the United Kingdom. Imagine my excitement when I discovered that within a month of my joining the company we were to embark upon a *three month* tour of major cities in the United States. I had never been away from home before, let alone abroad! All travel details were arranged with military precision, and our household was put into a complete flap when a letter containing final instructions arrived. We were to meet at The Savoy Hotel for a Press photo call prior to a transfer to Heathrow for our flight to Philadelphia. Gentlemen were to travel in a three-piece business suit and all ladies were to wear a formal suit, gloves, *and a hat*. I remember my first ever 'grown up' hat would not have looked out of place on the head of the late Queen Mother.

Touring America as a member of a highly regarded professional opera company was an amazing experience - we had wonderful audience response and invitations came to attend many fantastic receptions and galas. Life for me was about as glamorous as it could be. However, there was an occasional 'blip', which would bring me back down to earth. Licensing laws in the States were very, very strict and it was illegal to serve alcohol to anyone under the age of 21. I was 18. (I have to admit, I *looked* 14. However, we still tried it on.) After a show it was usual for a jolly gang of singers to find their way to a nearby hostelry for a general 'debrief'. The waiter or waitress would come over for our drinks order and my heart would sink when I heard: "Hi guys, what will you all be having... and how old is *that* one?" This happened with such monotonous regularity that my dear colleagues organised a rota so whenever we were rumbled, whoever's turn it was would simply shrug, stand up and accompany me back to the hotel. There we would order two glasses of hot milk from room service and wait for the others to return. I am ashamed to say I have been thrown out of more bars than any proper young lady should be prepared to admit. Mind you, I really did think they were taking things a little too far when I could not order the dessert in a very swanky restaurant overlooking Niagara Falls. With a plain vanilla ice in front of me, I could only look on enviously as all the others tucked into the house speciality - 'Peaches in Champagne'.

Christmas time that year found the company in Los Angeles, and the locals agreed it was unseasonably warm, even for them. To add to the totally surreal nature of the situation, we found ourselves doing a matinée performance on Christmas Day. The show was *Pirates of Penzance* - and the end of the first act finds the whole chorus in a secluded cove on the Cornish coast, executing a typical Gilbert and Sullivan dance routine (forward, side, together; back, side, together etc.). This twee little dance is rudely interrupted by the sudden arrival of Ruth (the pirate maid-of-all-work), and the assembled company scatter and hide in fear and horror. So, already in high spirits and bolstered by the anticipation of Christmas dinner in the sunshine, we embarked on our sedate little dance. Forward, side, together; back, side, together; forward, side, together; back, side, Oh dear... NO RUTH!! Fortunately, our dear maestro in the pit was no stranger to Christmas Spirit, and our predicament did not immediately faze him. He quickly signalled to the orchestra to repeat the phrase and we all soon twigged what was happening. And so began the nightmare when the music appeared to be on an interminable loop. Over and over again we shuffled our increasingly silly dance.   Meanwhile, the redoubtable contralto playing Ruth, Christene Palmer, was sitting in her dressing room, jacket off, feet up, enjoying a pre-prandial Christmas sherry with her dresser. She suddenly heard the Stage Manager over the tannoy system, his voice raised to a desperate whisper: "Ruth, Ruth - you're OFF!" In a blind panic, Christene leapt to her feet, grabbed her pirate hat and rammed it on her head (backwards). She raced down the corridor trying to fasten her jacket (all skew-whiff) and eventually rushed onto the set and fell in a heap in the middle of the now gently perspiring dancers. Instead of rushing off in terror to hide, everyone to a man stopped dancing and crowded round her prone, panting form and shouted: "HOORAY!" The curtain came down a little prematurely on a scene of near-pandemonium, but not before the puzzled audience was able to fully take in the sight of the pink, fluffy slippers that completed Ruth's bizarre ensemble.

On our return to the UK we continued to tour, rehearsing and adding in shows until we were performing the standard Gilbert and Sullivan repertoire of ten productions. (We only took five to America.) Very often we choristers would lose the thread as to which show was being performed until we reached the dressing room and saw what costumes were hanging on the rails. Once the rehearsal period for each new (to me) show was over and whenever we were performing in a town for a couple of weeks or more, I would find a local Secretarial Agency and offer my services as a 'temp' shorthand/typist for the coming week(s). I would regularly work in an office from 9 to 5 (9 to 1 on a Wednesday, which was a matinée day) and then sign in at the Theatre. On reflection, I can only put it down to the energy of youth, but it certainly served a purpose. Not only was I kept occupied during the day, my secretarial skills were being honed, and most importantly, I was able to afford to run my first car - a lovely green and white Triumph Herald.

The majority of our performances took place in large theatres, but occasionally an unusual venue presented itself. One such case was the De Montfort Hall, Leicester. Built as a large concert hall it could host conferences, concerts, fashion shows and even, I believe, boxing matches. As such, it did not possess the proscenium arch of a normal theatre (behind which are housed the stage curtains, or 'tabs'), and therefore a false proscenium arch had to be constructed. This meant that instead of disappearing up into the 'flies' (the roof space, from where scenery is 'flown' in) the tabs were hung as at a huge window and had to be opened and closed as if they were giant living-room curtains. Our first performance was a matinée of *The Mikado*. At the end of this show there is a 'picture call'. As the orchestra plays the last chord, the tabs come in and the cast swiftly arrange themselves into set positions. Immediately the tabs rise, thus creating the 'picture', before falling again. From then on, there would continue normal curtain calls. Due to the unusual curtain arrangement at the De Montfort Hall a chap from the venue had obviously been tasked with controlling the curtains from behind in case they billowed out and decapitated half the orchestra and front row patrons. The orchestra played the closing note of *The Mikado* and the curtains immediately swept across, with the de Montfort employee gamely hanging on to the upstage side of the thick fabric. As we quickly arranged ourselves into position for the quaint Japanese tableau we could see he was a very small man, dressed in a boiler suit and flat cap, and he did not look too happy with his part in the proceedings. Now, whether nobody had actually warned him; whether his mind was elsewhere; or whether he simply forgot we will never know, but as soon as he reached centre stage and the curtain immediately started back, in his confusion he just let go, standing transfixed like a rabbit in the headlights, stranded in the middle of the Japanese scene. Suddenly, as he realised his curtain was fast retreating back into the wings he snapped into action and with outstretched arms he performed a leap that would have made Rudolf Nureyev proud, disappearing into Prompt Corner virtually parallel to the stage. Needless to say, it was 'collapse of Japanese tableau'. Not unsurprisingly, his fifteen seconds of fame proved too much for him and we never saw him again. (Our Assistant Stage Manager carried out his duties for the rest of the run.)

When one is performing a relatively few shows over and over again it is very easy to lose concentration, and sometimes the wrong words inadvertently creep in. A salutary example of this was a particular performance of *Patience*. In this show, which has W.S. Gilbert poking fun at the pre-Raphaelite movement, all the ladies of the chorus are madly in love with a poet called Bunthorne and they spend most of the first act trailing around after him, hanging on to his every word. Towards the end of the act, another poet, Archibald Grosvenor, appears at the rear of the stage. He stands there in an 'aesthetic' pose until one of the ladies (Lady Angela) notices him and sings:

"But who is this, whose god-like grace
Proclaims he comes of noble race?"

- upon which all the other ladies turn upstage towards him, and decide he is far more attractive and interesting than Bunthorne, who is then promptly ignored. We subsequently spend the rest of the act trailing around after Grosvenor. Well, on this evening in question, we are all sitting adoringly at Bunthorne's feet when Peggy Ann (Lady Angela) turns and notices Grosvenor standing, with arms raised, ostentatiously 'reading' a book, towards the back of the set.

"But who is this, whose god-like grace
Proclaims he comes *from outer space*?"

- she trills. Not *hysterically* funny, I grant you - but it was enough to tickle the fancy of the ladies chorus that evening and we all turned upstage desperately trying to stifle our giggles, which naturally only made things worse. Unfortunately,

Kenneth Sandford, playing Grosvenor, had NOT heard the gaffe, and as far as he was concerned, the whole ladies chorus turned towards him, clapped eyes on him, and burst out laughing. He said it was the *worst* moment of his career. He was quite convinced his flies must have been undone - and having to remain in 'aesthetic' pose with book in hand, he could do nothing about it! It took several large gin and tonics in the bar afterwards before he would even speak to poor Peggy Ann again.

Towards the end of my second year touring with the D'Oyly Carte, and whilst we were playing the New Theatre, Oxford, an advertisement in *The Stage* for an 'open' audition for a new show to be produced at the Theatre Royal, Drury Lane caught my attention. I had recently got engaged to be married, so the prospect of a less peripatetic lifestyle was definitely appealing. There was only one problem - the audition was being held in London on the following Wednesday, a matinée day. Unfortunately, I am deeply ashamed to say, determination clouded my better judgement and so Wednesday found me driving down the A40 towards London, having phoned the New Theatre stage door pleading a 'tummy upset'. Although executing all subterfuge with utmost secrecy, I was still extremely nervous about being found out, and naturally quite stressed by the time I joined the queue of audition hopefuls at the stage door of the Theatre Royal.

It took a good couple of hours to eventually reach the side of the stage, by which time there was a great sense of camaraderie in the line, and although we passed the time chatting, I still could not bring myself to admit to anyone else that I was 'playing hookey'. Finally it was my turn and I strode onto the stage. I had just handed my music to the accompanist when a voice I recognised called out from the auditorium: "Glenys! Why on earth did you not tell me you were interested in this show? NEXT!!!" *It was John McCarthy*. On hearing the shouted "Next!" the Stage Manager automatically sent on another auditionee, so I could do no more than retrieve my music from the bemused pianist and stumble off into the opposite wings, where a couple of my new-found friends had been waiting to give moral support. "Poor you, they didn't even let you open your mouth", was the shocked whisper. I shrugged and managed a weak smile, but my stomach was churning. I had come all this way; told a Pinocchio-sized untruth, thereby jeopardising my perfectly good job - all to no avail. *What on earth could I have been thinking?*

It was one very chastened chorister who drove back to Oxford and signed in for the evening show. Luckily, my colleagues put my somewhat subdued mood down to having been 'poorly' earlier.

A week later, I received a letter inviting me to start rehearsals with the cast of *The Great Waltz*, which was to open at the Theatre Royal in the autumn.

ACT 1 - Scene 3

WEST END WENDY

Filled with glowing Strauss melodies, *The Great Waltz* opened at the world-famous Theatre Royal, Drury Lane to a rapturous reception. ("Sumptuously staged and beautifully sung" - Daily Telegraph.) Headed by international opera stars Sari Barabas and Walter Cassel, the producers (theatre impresarios Bernard Delfont and Harold Fielding) spared no expense in staging a show of unprecedented spectacle and glamour, created from much loved waltzes composed by both Johann Strauss I and Johann Strauss II. The story is loosely based on the real-life feud between the older and younger Strauss, allegedly because of the father's jealousy of his son's greater talent. The ball gowns worn by even the most humble chorine in the final scene were so magnificently extravagant and expensive that they were kept in a specially constructed tented 'dressing room' at the rear of the stage, and we were all required to come down to the stage in dressing gowns in order to don our fabulous creations. In contrast to many West End shows nowadays, there was also a generosity of participants. As well as a dozen principal artists (singers and actors), the twenty chorus singers were joined by a troupe of twenty dancers. When the curtain rose on the glittering final scene there was always a concerted gasp from the audience, followed by enthusiastic applause, as joining the fifty or so company members on stage was the entire orchestra, in full costume. The raising of the curtain on that scene never failed to thrill every single member of the cast.

If I were recounting the following very visual story in person, I would accompany the narration with a great deal of arm waving. So, dear reader, please bear with me as I attempt to translate a thousand gestures into much fewer than a thousand words.

The stage area of the Theatre Royal affords a huge barn of a space and houses one of the largest stage 'revolves' in the country. This can be used to great advantage when the set is changed: with a backcloth bisecting the centre of the revolve, a scene can be played out on the front half, whilst the stage furniture for the next scene is set on the back half. Then after dimming the lights, the front cloth comes down, the backcloth flies out and the whole stage revolves, whereupon another backcloth flies in. The front cloth is then flown out and lights go up on another scene to be played whilst the previous set is 'struck' (removed) and then re-set for the whole process to be repeated. This way a seemingly complicated scene change can take place in under a minute - a process that really reinforces the 'magic' of the theatre. One such dramatic scene change took place in the first act. A beautiful duet between Johann Strauss Snr and Helene Vernet set to the music of 'Tales from the Vienna Woods' takes place, naturally, in a picturesque clearing in the Vienna Woods. Several trees, a mossy bank sporting wild flowers and a trickling waterfall added to the romance of the scene. Towards the end of this duet as dusk begins to fall, the light fades, fireflies start to dance in the twilight and the two lovers wander, romantically entwined, into the wings. It is then that the stage crew springs into action. The front cloth comes in as the lights go down, the backcloth flies out, as do the trees, the revolve moves round - this time set with a long table and a few chairs - and another back cloth flies in. The chorus has been patiently waiting at the side of the stage ready to rush on and position themselves onto the new set. Immediately the front cloth flies out, the lights go up and we are plunged into the heart of a bakery (cue audience applause for an impressive scene change.) The next musical item is a big chorus number - the Radetsky March - to which has been choreographed a great dance routine. Only on one particular night, we are all positioned on set as the lights go up, just about to sing our first "Doodle-doot" of the Radetsky, when to our horror we see in the middle of the bakery an ENORMOUS tree which has unfortunately failed to be raised back into the flies during the scene change. Of course, we knew that in about ten seconds' time a troupe of twenty dancers would pile onto the stage, ready to perform an extremely complicated 'Busby Berkeley' dance routine. To see the poor dancers desperately trying to execute high kicks whilst dodging the huge errant tree meant that the Radetsky was rendered 'orchestra only' for that particular performance. (Phew! Only 480 words.)

The Great Waltz ran for an amazing and thoroughly enjoyable 2 years, after which I stayed in Theatre-land for a further year, transferring first to the Cambridge Theatre for Tom Brown's Schooldays and then to the Queens Theatre in The Card.

Tom Brown's Schooldays was a very interesting 'gig' as it was my first experience of 'booth' singing. The very nature of the story necessitated that the cast was predominantly young boys between the ages of six and eighteen. Strict laws governing the employment of children mean that, depending on age, a young person can only appear on the West End stage for a limited number of performances in a given period, so the cast was constantly changing. In order to maintain the highest musical standard, a small group of 'session' singers was booked to sing behind the scenes in the choral numbers. So for this show, six assorted singers sat in a windowless store area underneath the stage, ranged around a large wooden kitchen table. To this had been attached the essentials of our craft: six microphones, a video monitor trained on the conductor and a bare light bulb which, when lit, indicated that the mikes were live. Oh - and of course the most important items of equipment - a kettle, six mugs and a large tin of biscuits. Despite our somewhat basic accommodation, the boys loved to come and visit us on their way to and from the stage (cupboard love?) and we all enjoyed their youthful banter. Many of 'our lads' went on to make their names in the profession - Christopher Guard, Keith Chegwin and Simon Le Bon were all 'graduates' of Rugby School at the Cambridge Theatre. To while away the time when we were not actually singing (or eating biscuits) we would play silly games, such as holding mock auditions (the boys loved this one). Someone would elect to be the auditionee and sing a song, upon which the 'panel' would decide they were really looking for someone taller/shorter - so the singer would repeat the song on tiptoe/ hunched up. Then the panel would say they really needed a Cornish accent/ tap dancer/ drummer and so on, so the poor auditionee would attempt to incorporate these dubious attributes into his or her rendition, until usually a 'one-legged' performer fell over. One day David, our tenor, was reading *The Stage*, and he chanced upon an advertisement for an open audition for "Singers who could dance - an ability to play a musical instrument an advantage." Just up our street, we thought. We knew Bob, our baritone, could play the violin, so during the next few performances we feverishly rehearsed a routine, with Leila, Bob and I singing and dancing to fiddle accompaniment. Three for the price of one. Everyone, including the boys, was keen to add their two-pennyworth to some aspect or other of our presentation and eventually, very well rehearsed, the three of us presented ourselves at the Palladium Theatre for the afternoon audition session. It was really rather bizarre - all the people who had come to audition (and there were a couple of hundred) were invited to sit in the stalls and go up onto the stage in the order in which they were seated, so everyone was able to watch all the preceding performances. Sitting towards the rear of the stalls, we enjoyed quite an 'interesting' concert. I really would not want to be rude about fellow artistes, but after a while we concluded that these auditions had been timed very badly, and anyone who was even half-good must have been away working already. By the time it came to our turn and the three of us, rather snazzily dressed in co-coordinating black and white, trooped onto the stage, the atmosphere in the auditorium had morphed into Party Mode. Our loud Barber Shop rendition of an up tempo folk song, greatly enhanced by a slick dance routine and Bob's spirited Irish fiddle playing, had them dancing in the aisles - and garnered us a standing ovation. After our performance, a somewhat bemused Casting Director said that unfortunately they were not looking for 'Acts' on this occasion, but if we were interested in working on a cruise ship, to give him a call at the office later in the week.

Another aspect of this show that gave my family and me great excitement was that during the run, I understudied the actress Jill Martin, who was playing the role of Mrs Brown, (Tom Brown's mother). In her main scene, at the beginning of the show, she sings a duet with Squire Brown (Leon Greene) in a horse-drawn cart, accompanied by Tom and several 'daughters'. Of course, the inevitable happened and one day Jill succumbed to a nasty bout of flu. I was ON! After a week playing Mrs Brown, it did make everyone laugh when we realised that I was only eight years older than my eldest 'child'.

The Card, starring Jim Dale, Millicent Martin, Joan Hickson, Marti Webb, and Dinah Sheriden was one of Cameron Mackintosh's first West End shows. On its transfer from a Bristol Theatre Royal 'tryout' to the Queens Theatre, Shaftesbury Avenue, the producer decided to augment the 'dancers-who-can-sing' chorus with a few 'singers-who-can-get-away-with-the-impression-they-can-dance'. That is how Yvonne, Michelle, Roger and I joined a cast that had already been performing the show for several weeks in Bristol. Quickly, we had to learn all the musical numbers and were then taken well outside our comfort zone with a crash course in the dancing, choreographed by Gillian Lynne, no less. Luckily, they agreed our strongest suit was the singing - a talent definitely better executed whilst more or less stationary - so some interesting ways were devised for our characters to appear in a scene without drawing attention to the fact we were slightly more sedate in the more frenetic dance routines. I made a lovely wallflower at the Ball - and *someone* had to push a pram and wave a flag at the dockside. What a great show that was, packed full of hummable tunes (courtesy of Tony Hatch and Jackie Trent) and a very funny script by Keith Waterhouse. The whole cast really 'gelled' and we all had a great time in each other's company, both on and off stage. It was a horrible day when we came in to the Stage Door to be faced with a closure notice after 130 performances. The 'House Full' placard outside the Front of House compounded our distress - but we were later given to understand that the theatre had only been leased for four months, so we were on borrowed time anyway.

My next West End 'run' was in a totally different type of venue, and certainly was of unusual format. Next to Charing Cross station in the Strand stood a branch of the famous Lyons Corner House. The ground floor was a retail food hall, the first floor accommodated a self-service cafeteria, the second floor boasted a silver-service restaurant and the third floor offered private corporate dining rooms. There was even a nightclub in the basement (more of that later). Someone had the bright idea of converting the attic storerooms into what became a very successful tourist attraction: *Mediaeval Feestes* (sic). This enterprise involved the customers being welcomed at the door by a Master of Ceremonies 'Baron' and they were then ushered into his beautifully decorated Baronial Hall. There they were seated at long trestle tables, served a set mediaeval-themed meal by costumed serving wenches and entertained by members of the Baron's household - troubadours, minstrels, jugglers and a jester. This jollity, together with all the watered down cider you could drink included in the price of a ticket made for a very merry evening indeed. I was featured as the Baron's 'Page', and very fetching I looked, too. My hair was cut into a fashionable pageboy bob and my costume comprised a colourful satin (low-cut) doublet, gold lamé 'hotpants'(!) and beautiful red leather thigh boots. I would sit with the other entertainers at the top table to eat at the same time as the guests and would get up to sing a relevant solo or duet and/or interact with the revellers throughout the evening. The set menu was pea and ham soup (actually quite tasty) with rustic bread (often thrown, particularly at the jester); roast jointed chicken with vegetables; and a delicious lemon syllabub. At the time, I was newly married and my husband, Nick, worked for a large insurance broker in the City. I fell into the habit of taking home a 'doggy bag' with left over chicken pieces for Nick's supper the following evening. The poor man put up with this for nearly three months before he broached the subject; whilst he appreciated my valiant attempt at frugal housekeeping, he really could do with a change of menu.

Mediaeval Feestes proved very popular and we usually played to full houses of around 120 people on the Wednesday to Saturday opening nights. However, one Thursday evening the management called us all together to say they had taken in a block booking of nearly 200 patrons for the following night. A plan was devised. It was decided that the coat racks would be relocated into the hallway, allowing another trestle table to be set; extra places were to be laid at each table and the 'top table' would also be used for guests, so we entertainers were to take pot luck in the kitchen. An extra back-up barrel of cider had been ordered. These additional customers were somehow or other going to be accommodated: we *would* get them in. It was all very exciting and the Company arrived on the Friday in high spirits, prepared for an extremely jolly evening. Imagine our horror when it emerged that the management had omitted to tell us one important fact - our guests were all Scottish football supporters, down for an amateur Cup Final match at Wembley Stadium on the Saturday! AAARRGGHH!!!! However, despite all our misgivings we actually ended up having a really good time, and it taught me one very important thing: if you can stand dressed in gold lamé hotpants and red thigh boots in front of two hundred drunken Scottish football supporters - and sing 'Greensleeves' - you can sing *anything* to *anybody*.

Funnily enough, this new mantra was put into practice on a Saturday night a few weeks later, when the Manager from the Nightclub in the basement came racing upstairs in a panic. One of the three showgirls had slipped and sprained her ankle - could I possibly help out? Buoyed with the confidence of Youth and Ignorance, I agreed. The Nightclub operated on Friday and Saturday nights only and was a showcase for circuit comedians, magicians, and cabaret artists. The resident showgirls provided glamour by singing and dancing to introduce the acts. The headline act that weekend was comedian Don MacLean - and the girls were performing the song from *Sweet Charity* 'Big Spender'. The stage was tiny, so three girls filled it - but only two would have looked silly, especially with one singing the song and only one in the chorus. Another costumed body was needed, and if that body could sing along as well, that would be a bonus. So, after the show at the top of the building I made my way down to the basement where I was acquainted with my new work colleagues and was talked through a simple dance routine, which involved a small chair. The costume presented no problems - it was brief, but gorgeous (and I was already used to working in shorts and with a low décolletage.) A hairpiece was found to supplement my bob and, with the addition of several feathers, sparkly bits and bobs and an extra pair of false eyelashes, I felt I could almost get away with it. The shoes were a bit of a stumbling block though. I am a size 4½ and they were size 6: still, with the aid of a couple of sturdy elastic bands, I was ready to face the public. That first show went by in a bit of a blur and I was so grateful to have that chair to hang on to. I did my best, positioning myself just behind the other girl and following her movements as closely as I could. By the second weekend I really had got into the swing of it and was beginning to enjoy myself, singing lustily and draping myself in a sultry fashion over the chair. In fact I was really quite disappointed when the original girl's ankle healed and I found myself cast back into the Middle Ages upstairs.

FIRST INTERVAL

AND THEN I SANG

One of the great things about being a freelance singer is the infinite variety of 'gigs' that can come your way. We are like musical butterflies - flitting from one concert, broadcast, recording or show to another. Thankfully, I have always enjoyed learning new repertoire, so the prospect of something different was always appealing. Of course there is always the major downside to contend with - the offer of a more exciting and /or better paid job when you already have something in the diary. This is always a hideous dilemma and there is no easy solution, but from a purely personal position I have always felt it less stressful to bite the bullet and go with the original engagement. However, that does not stop the pangs of envy and thoughts of "if only..." when you see colleagues swanning off to do something you feel *you* would rather be doing. Fortunately, this has not happened to me too often - and on occasion those of us left behind have managed to capture an even better prospect whilst the 'A' team are out of the picture. Sometimes the angst of having to turn down an exciting proposition is totally self-inflicted. A friend was intending to attend an open audition for an extravaganza starring Danny La Rue which was being staged in the West End. Having nothing better to do that day, I said I would go with her to keep her company. Well, one thing led to another and I ended up singing too. To my surprise, they asked me to come back the next day and sing 'Everything's Coming Up Roses' from *Gypsy* - and I agreed. What was I thinking? I had a healthy looking diary with professional engagements for the next couple of months at least. There was absolutely no way I could commit myself to even a short run in a West End theatre. Despite this I returned and sang the requested song, which I had managed to learn overnight. I was then directed to see a lady who was stationed in the wings, who immediately whipped out a tape measure and started to measure me, obviously for a costume. "Hang on a minute", I blustered," I can't..." It was *SO* embarrassing and they were naturally not at all pleased that I had been clearly wasting everyone's time. I was mortified, even more so because by then I really thought it would be great fun to take part in the show. I took great care to see I never got into that awkward position again. (Incidentally, my pal *did* join the cast, and had a really enjoyable time.)

* * *

One of the most bizarre jobs I recall was a three week trip to Spain, where two colleagues and I were engaged to sing backing vocals for a Spanish pop singer. Juan Pardo was, at the time the number one pop star in his native Spain. My recollection of how we got the job, or even *why* has disappeared into the mists of time, but I remember that we were asked to prepare a three-part harmony pop song to perform as our solo spot at the concerts. We decided upon Stevie Wonder's 'You Are the Sunshine of My Life' and feverishly rehearsed this in the couple of weeks before the trip. Eventually Ann, Annie and I arrived at Madrid airport where a very pleasant man met us, although unfortunately he spoke no English. He drove us in a shiny black limousine to what we subsequently discovered to be a rather upmarket area in the centre of Madrid, whereupon he handed us the keys to a smart second floor flat and left us to our own devices. The next morning our driver picked us up and took us to a recording studio where we were introduced to Señor Pardo and the musicians in the band. The band members did not speak much English either, but they were a fun group of people, and together we set about learning and rehearsing our contribution to the band's concert set. After three days we were reasonably pleased with our progress and felt we ought to mention the 'solo spot' we had prepared, but to our surprise, blank incomprehension met every attempt to broach the subject. "Hooray!" we thought, "One thing less to worry about" - gleefully consigning Stevie to the bottom of our suitcases. On the third afternoon, Juan Pardo's American wife turned up and took us shopping for stage outfits. We were thrilled to be able to communicate easily with someone, but foolishly, we did not discuss with her more pertinent subjects, which we certainly would have done had we known that we would not see her again until nearly the end of the tour. Very late the next evening we were preparing to go to bed when the intercom to the flat buzzed. It was our driver. After a bit of a communications pantomime we eventually twigged that he had come to take us to our first performance. Hastily we got ready - the tour was on! Subsequent dates followed the same pattern: we were picked up late in the evening and driven for one, two, or three hours - without any real idea of where we were going. Performances took place in sports stadiums, campus halls, gymnasiums, arenas, and one particularly memorable venue was a shoe factory in Valencia. No performance started before 1 or 2am and every venue was absolutely packed. Usually driven home in the early hours of the morning, occasionally we stayed overnight, driving to even remoter parts of the country for the next show. One trip even involved an overnight train journey. As well as Valencia, I can recall visiting San Sebastian, La Corunna, Pamplona and Galicia, to name but a few. Eventually it came to our final show which took place in Madrid in a vast arena the size of Wembley Stadium. This was the only performance to take place before midnight, as Juan Pardo appeared to be the celebrity guest star at a 'Eurovision Song Contest' type competition, televised live throughout Spain. We had become used to fans mobbing him throughout the tour, but the appearance in Madrid took the excitement to a higher level, as Señor Pardo proved to be every bit as popular as The Beatles that evening. The next morning, heads still buzzing with exhilaration, we took our leave of our new Spanish friends and were taken to the airport, and home - still unsure as to why we were ever there in the first place.

* * *

Early in my musical career, there were many small opera companies (now sadly defunct, mainly due to financial constraints) touring and appearing in festivals etc. all over the country. I played the title role in Massenet's *Cendrillon* (Cinderella) for Opera Favorita at University College London, and Nella in Puccini's *Gianni Schicchi* at Brunel University, gaining invaluable solo stage experience. Opera 70 was a highly respected small company that regularly performed at the Chichester Festival, and it specialised in operatic rarities. *Justinus* by Legrenzi (1626-1690) was the first modern day performance of this opera, and it attracted a lot of attention from the opera cognoscenti who 'collected' rare opera performances. Totally opposite in date and style, the following year I played the title role in *The Lily Maid* by Rutland Boughton (written 1934), which also happened to be interesting to opera buffs. Playing Eufemia in *Justinus* proved to be most fortuitous for me as, a week before the opening night the girl playing the 'trouser role' of my brother Andronicus broke her leg and had to pull out of the production. Amazingly, the Musical Director managed to persuade Elaine Padmore to take on the role at incredibly short notice. An accomplished singer, Elaine learned the whole role in a few days, and she literally saved the show. However, the main reason for my good fortune was that Elaine was a lady of many talents (she later became Head of Opera at the Royal Opera), and at the time of the *Justinus* performances she was also Artistic Director of the prestigious Wexford International Opera Festival. Every year, for about six weeks in the late autumn, the small sleepy town of Wexford in Southern Ireland becomes vibrantly alive as opera lovers and performers from all over the world invade it. The operas staged are all outside the normal operatic repertoire - and both audiences and participants have a great deal of fun. Every conceivable public space is commandeered for practice and rehearsal, from meeting halls to the back room of a pub - and every time there are more than two people gathered together you can guarantee they are either talking about or singing opera. At Elaine's invitation I spent three very happy seasons 'doing' Wexford and I made many friends with whom I have remained in contact in the ensuing years. Of the half dozen or so operas in which I took part, I think the most memorable was *The Rise and Fall of the City of Mahagonny* (Kurt Weill). Six of us girls were engaged to play the roles of 'good time girls', and we were all assigned different characters and costumes. My character was 'Biker's Moll', and very fetching I looked too in my outfit of leather miniskirt, fishnet stockings, biker jacket and far too much eye make-up. So fetching, I attracted the attention of a certain Priest from the local Catholic Church, and I became aware that he had managed to wangle himself an invitation to virtually every social occasion the *Mahagonny* cast attended. He would sidle up to me and attempt to monopolise the conversation, with solicitous remarks as to how the 'Fallen Leather Lady' was today. When my colleagues noticed his unwanted attentions, I am afraid we treated it as a game and rather rudely made elaborate plans to avoid his company, particularly when he took to hanging around the Stage Door in the vain hope of escorting me home.

'FALLEN LEATHER LADY' RELAXING BACKSTAGE

One of Elaine's innovative ideas at Wexford was to establish the very popular 'Operatic Scenes'. Chorus members and those playing small parts on the main stage in the evening performances were invited to take part in short staged extracts and scenes from mainstream operas. These showcases, held in a spacious barn attached to the largest Wexford hotel, took place in the mornings and always attracted a packed and enthusiastic audience. This could have been due to the fact that, at best, Wexford was a 'one horse town' and it was inevitably raining, but I like to think that the audience was relishing a chance to pick out up-and-coming singers and directors. Of all the extracts I took part in over my three years at Wexford, the most memorable (for me) was Norina's Cavatina and subsequent duet with Dr Malatesta from Donizetti's *Don Pasquale*. This 'Scene' lasted around eleven minutes in total and proved to be a real tour de force for me. Staged 'in the round', with the audience on all sides, the set represented a small contemporary bedsit. As the scene opened I was discovered reading a novel, which is in accordance with the score (mine was a Mills and Boon romance, of course), but from then on the director went decidedly 'off-piste', and had me preparing a snack of beans on toast and a cup of tea, all in strict time with my singing. Looking through my *Don Pasquale* score, years later, I find a plethora of stage directions all set to coincide with certain chords or cadenzas: "Flap Bread", "Pop Up Toaster", "Open Tin", "Stir Beans", "Butter Toast", "Wave Spoon", "Drop Teabag In Cup", "Drink From Saucer" etc. etc. At the end of the scene I contrived to brush my hair, put on some lipstick, and change from dressing gown to outdoor coat, before rushing out and slamming the door at the exact time of the final chord. I doggedly practised the routine for hours on end, and even managed to rearrange the furniture in the front room of my digs to correspond exactly with the set, so I could practice getting the timing perfect (especially getting the toaster to pop up on the correct chord). Fortunately, I had a very understanding landlady.

* * *

Back home, I was one of the artists taking part in a Variety Show taking place in a large London Borough Town Hall. The performers had each been asked to introduce the subsequent act on the bill. In the second half, I followed an older gentleman doing a comedy magic act and during the interval he sought me out, as he was obviously concerned that he would introduce me correctly. My opening number for this spot was 'Love Live Forever' from Lehar's *Paganini,* so I carefully wrote this down on a piece of paper for him. Standing ready in the wings, I watched him take a bow at the end of his act and then remove my scrap of paper from his inside pocket with a theatrical flourish. "Ladies and Gentlemen" he announced, "Glenys will now sing for you....." There was a horrible silence as he paused, squinting myopically at the paper and patting his pockets in vain for non-existent reading glasses. Eventually he spoke: ".....Glenys will sing *PAGE NINE!*"

My travels took me also to a number of English seaside resorts at the behest of John Murphy, a very personable Irishman with an engaging stage presence and an attractive high tenor voice. He had amassed a considerable 'fan club' (mostly ladies of a certain age) for his regular series of shows, which took place at a dozen or so seafront theatres, in coastal resorts all the way from Great Yarmouth in Norfolk to Barnstaple in Devon. The format of these popular shows was invariably the same: the first half comprised three fifteen minute 'spots' from two guest artists (a baritone and a soprano or mezzo) and John's lady friend Joan (a tap dancing soubrette) and in the second half John took to the stage for forty five minutes taking spontaneous requests from the audience. A finale involving all participants, cobbled together at the brief rehearsal just before the show, concluded the evening. Throughout these entire proceedings, pianist Scilla Stewart would be sitting patiently at the grand piano on stage. Whilst she had printed music for the items in the first half, of course this was not feasible for John's ad hoc spot. One day I said to Scilla: "How come that you, a Kiwi who has only been in this country for a relatively few years, know all these obscure 'Old Time Music Hall' and Irish melodies?" She smiled and replied: "Oh, I don't - I just play what notes John sings, a split second after he has sung them." What an incredible talent!

I learned such a lot about performing from John Murphy. As well as giving me the incentive and opportunity to learn and present a vast repertoire or songs in such a variety of styles, he would always be willing to pass on words of advice and encouragement from his own impressive experience. "Always walk onto the stage as if you OWN it!" was a mantra I took on board. I have found it certainly does help to dispel nerves and create a rapport with the audience if you smile and LOOK confident!

* * *

By 1986 I had remarried and my husband Tony and I moved to The Lee, an idyllic Chiltern village, which gave me the opportunity to become involved in the flourishing local music scene. I became quite well known in the area, performing in concerts two or three times a year as part of the entertainment programme of The Lee Old Church and various other venues in the vicinity and regularly appearing as soloist with several neighbouring choral societies. It also seemed that no local church wedding was complete without a contribution from yours truly.

However, there were some 'proper' celebrities residing in The Lee and by hanging onto their coat tails I was able to become involved in some very interesting and enjoyable ventures, such as staged performances of Howard Blake's *The Snowman* with John Craven (of *Newsround* and *Countryfile* fame) as Narrator. Another notable 'local' was the distinguished actor Geoffrey Palmer and on one memorable occasion he invited several pals, including Dame Judi Dench, to perform in a starry Fund-raiser for the Simon Weston charity. Needless to say, I was thrilled to be asked to provide a vocal contribution to this glittering extravaganza. In accordance with tradition up and down the country, every two years The Lee put on a Pantomime, written and performed by local talent. Due to work obligations, neither Geoffrey nor I could ever commit ourselves to the entire week's run, but one year we both made special guest appearances, with Geoffrey as 'The White Rabbit' and me as 'Princess Diva'.

'THE WHITE RABBIT' and 'PRINCESS DIVA'

* * *

Friday Night Is Music Night is a long running BBC Radio 2 programme. Its format of light classical music and show tunes is still as popular today as it was when first broadcast 40 years ago. A singing group of a dozen voices usually joins the BBC Concert Orchestra and star soloists for a concert, which is broadcast live from the Hippodrome in Golders Green. I was fortunate to take part in the programme for many years as a member of two different groups - the John McCarthy Singers and the Charles Young Chorale. The Charles Young Chorale specialised in 'easy listening' arrangements - light pop songs sung in close harmony (Beatles tunes and Burt Bacharach etc.) whereas the John McCarthy Singers tended to take on the more classical repertoire. Indeed, for one memorable broadcast we found ourselves presented with the challenge of the 'Easter Hymn', from Mascagni's *Cavalleria Rusticana*. In the opera two full choirs, one on stage, one off stage, and a soprano soloist sing this piece. However, we were just twelve voices...and no soloist. During the all too brief afternoon rehearsal before the live broadcast, we struggled to allocate specific vocal lines to do the piece justice. In the end, John decided that everyone should attempt to sing *everything*. If in doubt - *SING!* Fortunately such mammoth tasks were rare, although that occasion did make several of our members look upon their *previous* bête noires - the Bus Medley or the Marrow Song (don't ask) - more fondly.

A spin-off from *Friday Night is Music Night* was *Songs From the Shows,* where *Friday Night* star soloists, together with the BBC Concert Orchestra explored the repertoire of Broadway and West End musicals. I was invited to take part as a soloist in several of these regular half hour programmes, teamed with *Friday Night is Music Night* favourites such as Ramon Remedios and Danny Street. The very best bit, I thought, was having my name in bold print in the Radio Times!

TALES FROM THE LODGE

I found myself on the books of a specialist Entertainment Agency, and from there I joined the 'Masonic circuit.' Most Lodges would book a pianist to play for the Master's Song during their dinner, and he would stay on to accompany my 15 minute singing spot after the meal. The fees were not brilliant, especially after the agent's commission was deducted, but I reckoned that if I was not doing anything else that evening it was a good excuse to dress up in one of my many glamorous concert frocks (thereby justifying the Schedule D tax relief) and a chance to try out new songs. Sometimes I would do two or three regular meetings a week. One evening my accompanist and I were outside one of the private dining rooms waiting for our call when the door to a dining room along the corridor opened and a rather flustered man came out. Seeing us, his face lit up. Were we scheduled to entertain his Lodge? We quickly ascertained that we were not: we were in fact, booked for an entirely different Lodge; but he was so crestfallen that we agreed to nip in and perform our programme to them first, as obviously his artists had not turned up. Double fees all round and a new client for the Agency - *result*!

I had a tried and tested format for my Masonic after dinner entertainment. When the Lodge was ready for us, my accompanist would go into the room alone and settle himself at the piano. Then he would play the introduction to my first song as I made my entrance, singing as I entered the room. One day I was booked to entertain a new (to me *and* to the Agency) Lodge. We surmised that they usually did the Master's Song unaccompanied, as the contract called both my pianist and me together at 8.30pm. We arrived at the unfamiliar venue in south London, got changed and waited outside the dining hall, as was our usual practice. Eventually we were summoned to appear and Martin, the accompanist, followed the Secretary inside, whilst I hovered behind the slightly ajar door, waiting to hear my introductory chord. I waited - and waited - until a good five minutes later a grinning Martin reappeared, followed by a red-faced Secretary. There was *no piano*! Apparently, as they had some very important visitors at that particular meeting, the Secretary had blithely booked a singer and pianist to entertain the Lodge, to make it a special occasion, but it simply had not occurred to him to check that there was a piano in the room - a rather important necessity for such entertainment. Martin said it had been one of the funniest scenes, with people lifting piles of coats and looking under dining tables in the vain hope of discovering a piano.

* * *

There was an occasion when I had unfortunately snapped a tendon in my calf and, of course, it was not at all a convenient a time for me to be 'confined to barracks'. As well as my chorus obligations at the Royal Opera House, I had several solo concerts in the diary including a Masonic 'Ladies Night', so I embarked on an intense course of ultra-sound and physiotherapy so I could get back on track (and stage) as quickly as possible. I managed to get back into *The Magic Flute*, which is quite a static show for the chorus, by reaching the wings on crutches, leaving these with one of the Assistant Stage Managers, and hopping onto the stage at the back with the support of a colleague. Leaning on said colleague, I then sang the chorus and hopped off again. The solo concerts were quite a different matter. Obviously my ability to sing had not been affected, so I telephoned the person in charge and explained the situation. I was perfectly willing and capable of performing for them, but "*I would be on crutches*". If they considered this a problem, I would endeavour to find a suitable substitute singer and they would have to release me from my contract. Fortunately, they all professed to be more than happy for me to perform and I managed the first two concerts very well. I even dressed up my crutches with co-ordinating ribbons to match my concert frock, which I thought was quite a nifty idea. However, at the third venue (the Ladies Night), the person who welcomed me was quite unable to hide his discomfiture and horror at the sight of my tastefully decorated walking aids. "But, you're *on crutches*!" he cried. "Well, yes" I said, "I *did* explain my predicament to you over the telephone, and you said you were perfectly happy for me to continue with the contract. After all, it's my <u>leg</u> that is poorly, not my voice." "Oh yes, I <u>know</u> you said you were 'on crutches', but... but...but.... I didn't expect you to be using a CRUTCH!" was his somewhat bewildering reply. (In the event, the performance went very well, and everyone else was very nice about it.)

GREMLINS AT GRIMSDYKE

'Grimsdyke' is a large country house set in beautiful and extensive grounds, located near Stanmore, North London. It was originally owned by W.S. Gilbert (the wordsmith half of the famous Gilbert and Sullivan duo.) Most weekends, G & S aficionados would visit to enjoy a tour of the house and grounds, followed by a lavish afternoon tea or dinner in Gilbert's gracious drawing room, and a group of singers (mostly ex D'Oyly Carte members) would perform songs and excerpts from the G & S operetta repertoire between the courses. As the 'Lord High Understudy' for the soprano in the team, I was regularly called upon to take part in these performances. These proved to be very popular 'gigs' as, dressed in appropriate Victorian costume, we would dine with the guests, and the delicious afternoon tea or three course dinners definitely enhanced the fee. One evening there was a new chef in the kitchen and he was really striving to impress. The meal was even better than usual, and by the time we reached the dessert course we could not believe our luck. The most delicious looking concoction appeared before us. A generous sized milk chocolate cup, filled with a rich white chocolate mousse, smothered by a thick dark chocolate sauce.... Yum! All four singers greedily gobbled up every last morsel of the chocolate heaven. The first number in our final set was 'Regular Royal Queen', a quartet from *The Gondoliers*. Each singer has a solo verse, followed by a short chorus. As 'Gianetta', I was the first to sing. "Then one of us will be a queen, And - gurgle - gurgle - gurgle - " Help! My vocal cords felt completely clogged by a surfeit of chocolate. I struggled resolutely through my verse, sounding more and more like Donald Duck, with my three colleagues smirking and giggling behind me. Next up was the tenor, 'Marco'. "She'll ride about in a carriage and pair, With - gurgle - gurgle- gurgle - ".

"Ha Ha! Serves you right", I thought, stifling my own laughter. Then it was the turn of the mezzo, 'Tessa'. "Whenever she condescends to walk, Be sure she'll - gurgle - gurgle - gurgle- ". By the time the baritone, 'Guiseppe' had made his futile attempt, we were all practically helpless with laughter. Soon our audience - well aware of the cause of our predicament - were laughing with us. The chef was instructed to take chocolate off the menu in future.

Occasionally we were required to give a 'private' performance to small Corporate or Tour groups. On one such evening, after being shown round the house, a tour bus of Japanese visitors were ushered into W.S. Gilbert's private sitting room for a short concert. This pretty room was relatively small, so dressed in our Victorian finery, we were standing and singing in very close proximity to our audience. Every single member of the group had a large SLR camera hanging round their neck (this was well before the advent of iPhones and Instagram), and as we commenced our programme they started snapping away. No one seemed the *slightest* bit interested in the singing, and soon they were all lining up, taking individual and group photographs with us *whilst we were actually performing*. It was the most bizarre experience, trying to maintain the professional status quo, whilst being jostled, albeit politely (lots of bowing), with flashbulbs exploding all around. At one point a chap was actually lying at my feet, presumably to get a more 'interesting' angle. However, the moment we stopped singing, they all bowed very low and trooped out to board the coach. All singers are naturally very wary of being photographed whilst performing (mouth wide open is never a good look) and I shudder to think what celluloid horrors resulted from that evening.

ACT 2 - SCENE 1

AMBROSIA!

One of the best things about working for John McCarthy's Ambrosian Singers was the infinite variety of jobs. One day you were backing a rock musician (Rick Wakeman, or The Electric Light Orchestra for example) and the next you could be singing Verdi or Puccini choruses with Luciano Pavarotti or Placido Domingo. Very often, you did not know who you were working with until you reached the rehearsal room or recording studio. A prime example of this was when, one Monday morning, we were called to a small recording studio in Barnes, south west London. Patrick, one of the more mature members of the Ambrosians had arrived very early and was in the green room where the usual tea and coffee making facilities were available. He had put the kettle on to boil when an unfamiliar lady joined him. Assuming her to be a member of the recording studio staff, he somewhat cheekily indicated the now boiling kettle and said: "Mine's white with one sugar." Charmingly, the stranger smiled and made them both a cuppa, before disappearing into the studio. An hour later, when we had all assembled in the recording studio ready to start, Patrick's face was a complete picture when the recording engineer came out of the control booth, and introduced Patrick's 'tea lady'. It was Barbra Streisand! Unaware that the day's sessions were for her film *Yentl*, he had failed to recognise her.

Another time, a group of about twenty of us were all rather bemused by the music that had been handed out on arrival at the studio. There did not seem to be much of a tune, or even words. At one point, we all stood in a circle around a microphone, and *wailed* - high and low, loud and soft, for several minutes on end. Not many straight faces at the end of that afternoon. Eventually the record producer seemed satisfied with our contribution and wished us all a safe journey home. One of the girls rummaged in her handbag for her car keys, but on retrieving them, dropped them in total shock. Her Yale front door key was twisted into a perfect spiral! At that point the producer came out of the control box and announced that we might be interested to know that the recording session had been for Uri Geller. The mangled key was produced for inspection by the now shaking soprano. Completely unfazed he answered, quite matter-of-factly, that this often happens where Mr Geller is involved, and he would be very happy to pay for the cutting of a new key. This story is absolutely true... *I WAS THERE!!!*

* * *

The made-for-TV operas, of which there were about a dozen productions, took several weeks of rehearsal and recording sessions, as this time we had to memorise the score, which was a distinct change from our usual 'rehearse, record, and move on' style of work. Rehearsal venues were usually draughty and dingy church halls or Territorial Army Drill Halls in and around London. Rehearsals for *The Count of Luxembourg* took place in 'The Galtymore Ballroom', a somewhat euphemistically named Irish Social Club located on the Cricklewood High Road, North London. Although the BBC Stage Managers did sterling work in trying to get the rehearsal space habitable before each rehearsal, there was always a very strong smell of stale cigarette smoke and Guinness about the place, especially first thing in the morning. I will always cherish the memory of the extremely elegant and glamorous Adele Leigh emerging from her chauffeur-driven Rolls Royce in a fabulous full length mink coat, and then picking her way gingerly through the bar, negotiating the tables still covered with discarded glasses and full ashtrays - the floor sticky with spilt beer.

It was always exciting when the rehearsal period ended and we transferred to the main television Studio 1 at the BBC, Wood Lane. We thoroughly enjoyed spending a great deal of time 'star spotting' in the corridors around the studios and the Staff Canteen. By then, of course, we were ourselves in costume and make up and became objects of curiosity for others working at the BBC. The costume and make-up required for one particular opera, Verdi's *Macbeth*, caused a great deal of hilarity. As witches, the ladies chorus was identically dressed in black rags and we all had hideous masks with gauze-covered eye sockets, large hooked beak-like noses, pronounced bald foreheads, and sporting feathers for 'hair'. The only bit of us on show was our mouths, and the make-up girls painted these with jet black lipstick. One of our number was a real 'glamour puss' and was very unhappy about her appearance. The make-up supervisor ticked her off when she was caught adding lip-gloss over her black lipstick. My friends Hillie, Leila and I were having so much fun that we decided we needed a photograph to record these costumes. Spotting the on-set stills photographer in a brief moment before the next 'take', Leila and I grabbed Hillie and posed for a commemorative photograph. Later that afternoon, Hillie came over and said: "When are we going to get our photo taken?" She was less than impressed when it turned out that Leila and I had mistakenly included Ann-Marie in our group photo instead of her.

WHICH WITCH?

Whilst filming *La Traviata*, the props department had gone to town in the party scene, with a sumptuous banquet of delicious looking finger food laid out on the buffet table. It was pointless telling a large group of singers that it was only for show and should not be touched "for continuity reasons". Singers are a notoriously greedy bunch of people; soon vol-au-vents and sausage rolls were being snaffled surreptitiously, with the remaining items being moved around the plates to disguise the empty spaces. It was only after several singers complained of tummy-ache that it was revealed that, in accordance with safety regulations, the whole spread had been liberally sprayed with a fire retardant!

We were often booked to provide the 'vocals' in television plays - usually off camera, but sometimes in vision. One such time was in the mini-series *Shoulder to Shoulder* about the Suffragette movement, which starred Sian Phillips. A small group of us learned various Suffragette Anthems and, as 'extras' we appeared in several episodes - leading the live singing or miming to pre-recorded backing tracks, as required by the action. In one episode, Leila and I were none too happy about how we looked (something to do with our less than flattering wigs, if I remember rightly.) We decided that we really did not want to appear on television looking so frightful, so we were very careful to position ourselves at the back of the set, well behind the rioting hordes of Suffragette colleagues in front of the cameras. All was going well until suddenly we heard the director call over the tannoy system: "Camera 4, move to the rear. I want a close up of the girls at the back..."

One day, the BBC asked for three sopranos to provide a backing track for a television play set mainly in a boys' boarding school. I think it must have been the school holidays and the producer could not get actual boy choristers at short notice. Anyway, the three of us multi-tracked a couple of songs in our very best choirboy voices. The morning after the transmission, we were doing the regular church service at the Carmelite Priory and having a coffee in the crypt after the rehearsal, as usual. The lady parishioner who served us coffee was waxing lyrical about the "wonderful young boys singing on the television last night." "Oh yes", said Lynda, "That was me, Alison and Glenys." But nothing, not even when we sang for her the complete repertoire from the television show 'in character', would convince her that we had been involved.

Watership Down was another television sound track being recorded in the August school holiday period. The producer, Mike Batt, suddenly asked John McCarthy if he could provide a boy treble to sing a solo. John, thinking on his feet, remembered that alto Shirley Minty's son had won a choral scholarship, so he turned to her and asked if his voice had broken. "I do hope so", she replied: "he's 29 now." Collapse of all within hearing distance.

* * *

Although we took part in many concerts broadcast on radio, such was the reputation of the Ambrosian Singers that we regularly received invitations to perform in one-off galas and festivals throughout Europe. One such occasion was a performance of *The Messiah* in Perugia, Italy. The chorus all brought their own well worn scores to the rehearsals. The conductor was scheduled to fly in from Berlin to take the final piano rehearsal, but his plane was delayed. This necessitated John McCarthy conducting what, for the Ambrosians, was an entirely superfluous rehearsal. Eventually, towards the very end of the session, the conductor arrived. He listened for a few minutes, and then said: "You sing in English? The soloists sing in German!" Taken aback, John answered: "We don't have German language Messiah scores in England" then turned to us and said, conspiratorially: "Not too clear with the diction folks, perhaps they won't notice."

The Ambrosian Singers were a particular favourite of the celebrated Italian conductor Claudio Scimone, the founder of I Solisti Veneti, and on several occasions we travelled to Italy to take part in concerts and recordings with this renowned orchestra. Under Maestro Scimone's baton, performances took place at the iconic Teatro Olimpico in Vicenza, and in Venice the exquisite Teatro La Fenice and even the world famous St Mark's Basilica. One memorable concert was a performance of Rossini's rarely performed work *Zelmira* at La Fenice. Maestro Scimone had gathered together a stellar cast of international soloists for the main roles in this opera (Chris Merritt, Cecilia Gasdia etc.), but a small role had been offered to Ambrosian tenor Vernon Midgley. We, his humble colleagues, had been thrilled to see Vernon's name in large print on all the advertising posters, liberally displayed all around Venice. However, after the final run-through on the afternoon of the performance, the Maestro realised that the concert was in danger of seriously over-running. He spoke with Vernon and informed him that, due to time constraints he was making a necessary cut to the score. Unfortunately, this cut encompassed virtually all Vernon's role, leaving him with just one little section of a few bars to sing. During the performance Vernon sat patiently at the end of the line of soloists waiting for his big moment. Counting the bars before his entrance Vernon prepared to stand up to sing. *Too late!* The orchestra seemed to "take off like a bat out of hell" (according to Vernon) and before he could open his mouth the section was over. He had not sung a note. The poor man just had to sit back down again, much to the amusement of his 'friends' behind him in the chorus. I don't think he ever did live that one down.

Sometimes visiting conductors were not aware of the advantages of using professional choristers. I remember an absolutely stunning performance of the Verdi *Requiem* at The Royal Albert Hall, where the conductor, more used to the massed voices of amateur choirs, had insisted that the Promoter hired *two hundred* singers for the chorus. John's address book was seriously plundered and I imagine that just about every professional singer in London was on stage at the Albert Hall that night. What a fantastic evening that was, especially the 'Dies Irae'. Definitely one for the Special Memory Box.

With the major opera houses closed for the holiday season, the bulk of our opera recordings took place in the summer months, when the main recording companies could line up their biggest stars for complete 'box set' opera recordings. EMI, Decca, CBS and Phillips would assemble their 'dream team' of soloists (Pavarotti, Domingo, Scotto, Freni, Caballe etc. etc.), accompanied by one of our most prestigious orchestras (Philharmonia, or London Symphony Orchestra), conducted by Muti, Abbado, Levine etc. etc. Fortunately, the Ambrosian Singers were usually the chorus of choice and we were privileged to be part of some of the most prestigious and amazing music-making imaginable. However, not everyone was impressed. One of the most exciting recordings (and certainly the loudest) I ever took part in was *Ivan The Terrible* by Prokofiev. The conductor was Ricardo Muti, a tremendous musician, well known to be a strict disciplinarian. He could silence a rowdy orchestra and chorus with a single look. We were all assembled in Kingsway Hall, central London - an augmented Philharmonia Orchestra of 160 players, choir of 80 singers and a vast line-up of stellar Russian soloists. The red light was on, indicating a live recording, when a few of us became aware that a door at the side of the hall, which led out into the street, had been pushed open. In strode a tough looking man in a flat cap. Totally oblivious to the cacophony of sound around him, he surveyed the scene and decided that the man in charge was obviously the one standing on a podium waving a stick. As he marched determinedly towards the Maestro, the orchestra and chorus gradually fell silent. Everyone was holding their breath in horror as he said: "'ere, is that your van outside? It's blocking the entrance and I can't get me van past. You're going to have to move it, mate." The whole place then collapsed with laughter and even Muti had to smile.

I have such wonderful memories of Ambrosian sessions and concerts - but I think two have really stood out over the years. The first special memory is the last session of the *Ivan the Terrible* recording. The Philharmonia had drafted in even more players to cope with the score of the final scene. Several racks of tubular bells were ready to be hammered by a particularly enhanced timpani section. One set was so huge that the timpanist could only attack them from the top of a stepladder. The brass section was so large it was like a brass band convention. The guys in the recording booth told us to "go for it" - and "go for it" we did! The sound was deafening, yet so exhilarating at the same time. Maestro Muti whipped everyone up to a wild frenzy and the last note of the piece seemed to go on forever. When the red light went out at the end, there was an amazing feeling of achievement throughout. Then the recording engineer announced that it was the loudest single take ever recorded on EMI's equipment and we could not *possibly* run the excerpt again. A one take wonder!! We all went home on a high that night and I can still recall the feeling when I play the recording at home.

The other magical moment occurred during a recording of *Lucia di Lammermoor* (Donizetti) in Studio 1, Abbey Road Studios. In this opera, the 'Mad Scene' is a real tour de force for a coloratura soprano and one of my favourite sopranos, the much underrated Edita Gruberova, was singing Lucia. The forty-strong chorus was sitting at the far end of the large studio behind the line up of soloists, as this charming yet unassuming lady started to sing. As the scene progressed -it lasts about 17 minutes - we all became more and more captivated by the beauty and eloquence of her singing. Her coloratura was brilliant - crystalline notes of unerring accuracy complemented the wonderful warmth and tone of the legato phrases. By the time she reached (and held) the last note - a stunning top E flat - every single member of the choir was sitting on the edge of their seat not daring to breathe. The red light went out and there was total silence in the studio, for several long seconds. Then, as one, the whole chorus *and* orchestra rose to their feet and spontaneously burst into wild applause. Edita seemed genuinely surprised by this outburst, smiled shyly, and started to head towards the Control Box at the other end of the studio. She had to walk through the entire orchestra and the clapping continued for several minutes, until well after she had disappeared from view. I had never seen this amazing reaction, either before or since, from hard-bitten orchestral players and session singers, acknowledging and respecting an exceptional talent. Another one take wonder, and a Magic Moment indeed.

THE AMBROSIAN SINGERS BEFORE A CONCERT AT THE ROYAL FESTIVAL HALL 1990

PAUSE (SCENE CHANGE)

LIONHEART

And now for something completely different...

It was a dark, wet and miserable evening in late February 1979. In our home in Seer Green, Buckinghamshire - Nick, Monko (my mother-in-law), the two beagles (Bytum and Barley) and I were cosily ensconced in Monko's sitting room watching television. Suddenly the telephone rang and I picked up the receiver.

"Could I speak to Glin please?" a very high pitched and distinctive voice enquired.

"Glin, um, sorry, Glenys speaking...."

"Oh, hello Glin - this is Kate Bush here...."

A long silence from me - until (I thought) the penny dropped.

"Oh come on, Hillie - that's the worst impression I've ever heard you do!"

"Oh no, it is - Reeeely."

...."Really?"

One of the most memorable and enjoyable episodes in my career very nearly came to grief at the first hurdle - as I thought it was my friend Hillie playing a practical joke.

Fortunately Kate (for it definitely was she) managed to convince me and I agreed to drive over to her home in South London the next evening.

Kate was riding high in the pop charts at the time. Her single 'Wuthering Heights' with its quirky high vocal line and 'ear worm' catchy tune had burst onto the music scene and garnered an enormous fan base. Her first album *The Kick Inside* proved phenomenally successful and she had a new album *Lionheart* to promote. She was about to embark on a UK and European tour.

Gordon Farrell was a bass baritone who sang with the Ambrosian Singers and, as he lived near Kate in South London, I believe she had been to him for voice coaching. As the tour planning became more advanced, Kate asked Gordon's advice when it became obvious that an unusually wide vocal range for the backing vocalists would be required if the songs on the albums were to be faithfully reproduced 'live' on stage. (Kate did all her own backing vocals in the recording studio - overdubbing both very high and very low pitched effects.) Gordon suggested that classically trained singers would be the best option and, to my immense good fortune, he passed my phone number on to her. (At that time I was in my twenties and one of the younger - and dare I say, more 'with it' members of the Ambrosian Singers - which is probably why Gordon identified me as being a suitable candidate.)

So, there I was, sitting on Kate Bush's sofa, drinking herbal tea and playing with her two adorable cats, Pyewacket and Zoodle. I honestly cannot remember whether I actually sang anything or not, but I obviously convinced Kate that I had the vocal range needed and I could reproduce the sound she wanted. I realise now it was vitally important that she liked me as a person and that she felt I would fit in with the rest of the band. Hooray! I was invited to join the *Lionheart* Tour and tasked with finding an 'accomplice' B/V (Backing Vocalist), starting on Wednesday.

Liz Pearson was a 'free spirit' - a rather more experienced colleague - who I worked with on recordings and concerts for the Charles Young Chorale. Also classically trained, we went to the same singing teacher, Eduardo Asquez. Liz was good fun, a good singer and we got on well. This was important, as we were to spend the next few months working and living together very closely. To my total relief and delight, Liz jumped at the chance to spread her wings and do something totally different.

Somewhat nervously we presented ourselves at Shepperton Studios, where we joined the rest of the band, Stewart and Gary the dancers and Simon the magician. This was somewhat daunting as the band had been working together very closely for a couple of months and had already 'gelled'. However, it soon became clear that we would all get along. Kate had chosen well. There evolved a wonderful sense of professional camaraderie, with lashings of mutual respect and admiration but overall a glorious sense of fun. I do not think I have ever laughed so much, or enjoyed the company of a group of musicians as I did on the *Lionheart -Tour of Life*. Paddy, Ben, Preston and Brian all possessed a particularly witty sense of humour and could (and did) provoke fits of giggles at every opportunity.

But we had a show to get on the road (literally!). Kate worked closely with Liz and me, singing through each number we were to be involved in, demonstrating what we were to sing and where. I do not recall much printed or handwritten music (quite a departure for a 'session' singer) so we probably wrote our own word cues to help with the memorising. Naturally we had to sing everything from memory, so we would have discarded any bits of paper pretty quickly. Between us, Liz and I shared out the harmonies, and in extremis I ended up with the top B's and C's and Liz commandeered the bottom G's. All most satisfactory. The show was evolving into something quite extraordinary and really rather revolutionary for its time. Much less a standard 'pop' gig, it was a highly choreographed and professionally staged production, involving specialist lighting and sound effects, myriad costume changes, props, magic and dance. Most of the numbers Kate danced, whilst singing live, aided by a 'new-fangled' head mike, although occasionally she sat at a grand piano (for a rest?) and accompanied herself in a song. As a daring departure from the norm, Kate did not address the audience at all during the show, as each number flowed into the next with carefully rehearsed links by band members, the dancers, or Simon the magician. The only difference in these rehearsals from those for a West End theatre or opera production was that, in accordance with 'rock' culture, nothing happened in the morning. We would start work around three in the afternoon and carry on until the wee small hours. After a week or so of intensive rehearsing we moved to the famous Rainbow Theatre in Finsbury Park for run-throughs and dress rehearsals. The intense cold inside and the discarded debris of the previous night's extravaganza (Bill Haley and the Comets no less) very swiftly dispelled the anticipated glamour of working in such an iconic building. Eventually we reached the final dress rehearsal stage. This was so exciting - and I feel sure everyone on stage then realised that we were involved in something entirely new and innovative, a complete barnstormer of a show, which would turn the world of pop and rock tours on its head.

Kate was absolutely amazing - she was on stage throughout the entire show, singing and dancing, with only a quick dash into the wings to change costume between each number. Her stamina, both physical and vocal, was quite phenomenal. Kate's ability to pitch accurately the beginning of songs without any discernible introduction impressed me. I did suspect that she has perfect pitch, but unfortunately never got round to asking her. She had an enviable natural vocal style - something I appreciate even more now that I teach young singers myself. Her vocal production did not rely on the chest register, so beloved of the current crop of pop singers (which can be potentially damaging if abused).

Well done, Gordon! She always sang in tune on live performances - again this is a natural asset that sets her apart vocally (no auto-tune available in 1979!).

At last the rehearsal period was over and we embarked on the sell-out tour of the UK and Europe which involved shows in Stockholm, Copenhagen, Hamburg, Amsterdam, Stuttgart, Munich, Cologne, Paris, Mannheim and Frankfurt. The planning was meticulous. Hotels were booked, transport arranged and, before the 4pm 'Sound Check', a veritable vegetarian banquet was laid on at each venue for cast and crew - provided by "We Stuff The Stars" - and they certainly did! As well as ensuring all participants were well fed - essential for the stamina and fitness levels required for such a gruelling tour - this enabled the musicians and stage crew to socialise. This greatly enhanced the tight-knit 'family' atmosphere of the whole team. Probably the most challenging aspect of the whole project was to set up and run the show in such diverse venues - often with only a one day 'turn around' between performances. Not only different types of venue (theatres, concert halls), but also in different countries. A logistical nightmare! Looking back, I can see that the stage crew and sound and lighting engineers were absolutely fantastic and obviously right at the top of their game. We are talking 35 years ago - no computer designed and programmed lighting and sound boards then. The more I think about it, the more I am in awe of the guys who managed to produce such an amazing show, night after night. After each performance the stage crew swung into action for the 'get out'. They were usually assisted by 'humpers'. These were burly lads recruited from the immediate area and more often than not the local Chapter of Hells Angels. I remember one particular evening, after the show at the New Theatre Oxford, there was a very much larger than usual contingent of fans still crowding around the stage door a good hour after the show had ended. Richard, the Company Manager was rather concerned that a potentially dangerous situation presented itself. We (and particularly Kate) could be mobbed by well meaning but over-enthusiastic fans whilst transferring to the coach waiting to convey us all back to the hotel. So instead of exiting the stage door at leisure, signing programmes (!) and moseying onto the coach as usual, we were all instructed to wait behind the stage door until *everyone* was ready to leave. The humpers of the evening (a particularly striking and terrifying bunch of Hells Angels) were temporarily relieved of their humping duties and brought down to form a human chain corridor. At a given signal, the door was flung open and we all made a mad dash for the coach, which promptly shut its door the moment the last person hopped aboard. Richard's fears had been well placed. I scrambled into a seat and found myself confronted by a sea of faces pressed up against the coach windows. Dozens of fans had managed to climb *onto* the coach itself and were hanging, some upside down, waving, shouting and laughing. We all breathed a sigh of relief and, from the safety of our upholstered chariot, waved, shouted and laughed in reply.

Back at the hotel, after every performance there was communal 'wind down' time. Quite often a separate hotel room had been booked, specifically to accommodate those members of the company who were too 'hyped' to go straight to bed. We would congregate there, drink copious amounts of tea and pester room service for cheese and tomato sandwiches and biscuits. These usually disintegrated into hysterical joke-telling sessions, until tired by the late hour (usually 2 - 3am) or exhausted from laughing, we would gradually drift off back to our own rooms. Sometimes after a show, some sort of entertainment or reception had been specially arranged. Meals at local restaurants were often accompanied by a crowd of fans who had managed to follow the coach and would sit outside peering wistfully through the window. One night, when we were dining in an exclusive fish restaurant in Edinburgh, it was so cold that Kate felt sorry for them, and so she took out a bottle of wine and signed some photos. It turned out that they had travelled all the way from Coventry to see the show!

Two 'after the show' incidents stand out in my memory. The first, in Paris, was being taken to the famous Paris Lido where we enjoyed a show of incredible glamour and glitziness. Only at the end of the performance did I realise that the majority of the gorgeous creatures on stage were young men. Then, in Hamburg, we had a grand reception to celebrate the *Lionheart* tour and the organisers had had the brilliant idea of making the centrepiece on the buffet table a huge lion sculpted in butter. Unfortunately, they had underestimated our sense of fun and in no time the lion had pretzel whiskers, stuffed olive eyes and a lolling tongue fashioned from a slice of ham.

There was, out of necessity, a lot of travelling time between venues. In the UK this was on the 'Band Coach' which was equipped with all the latest mod cons, including a small television and a cassette deck (wow!) Listening to music was a favourite for long journeys and I was delighted to be introduced to so many interesting artists. Gino Vanelli, Ricky Lee Jones and Janis Ian remain favourites to this day.

We finished the UK tour with a week's residency at the London Palladium, and when we returned from the European tour we performed extra shows at the Apollo, Hammersmith, where we recorded a video of some of the numbers in the show. A few months after the tour we reunited to record a Christmas Special for BBC2 at Pebble Mill studios. Peter Gabriel and Steve Harley joined us in the studio and Liz and I were thrilled to perform backing vocals for both these major stars. However, I think my best memory of the whole tour happened in the Staff Canteen at Abbey Road Studios. Kate and I were sitting together having a coffee during a break in rehearsals for the Christmas Show, when none other than my childhood idol - Cliff Richard, joined us.

"Ooh, Cliff - have you met my friend Glin?" she said.

Yesssss!!!!!!

ACT 2 - SCENE 2

THE SILVER SCREEN AND TV 'GOLDEN OLDIES'

It always created a frisson of excitement when we were booked for a film session because you never knew what to expect. Some films involved singing works from the standard classical repertoire, for example lots of Mozart for *Amadeus*; Suo Gan (a Welsh folk song) in *Empire of the Sun* and Jerusalem in *Chariots of Fire*. Other film soundtracks I have sung on have gone on to become 'standards' in their own right, such as Vangelis' extraordinary score for *Chariots of Fire* and Ennio Morricone's *The Mission*. Considered to be the greatest composer of film scores of all time, John Williams has opened up a completely new genre of popular classics with his thrilling and tuneful scores for the *Superman* and *Star Wars* films. I think it is safe to say that we all knew something very innovative and special was happening in the studio on a John Williams film session.

When a singer is required to sing in a foreign language, with standard European languages (French German, Italian) the words would be written out correctly, as professional singers do acquire a basic knowledge of how to pronounce these languages over time. However, for other languages (e.g. Russian, Czech, Welsh etc.) the lyrics are usually written phonetically. This is also the case when basic sounds (ooh's aah's eee's etc.) are wanted for a special effect in a film score. On one John Williams film session we were presented with a song with phonetically written words, but nobody could quite work out which language they represented. Eventually one of our number (there is always one) announced most authoritatively: "Ah yes! It's *Turkish*!" We were all most impressed, and in our very best Turkish accents we all proceeded to slowly chant, in accord with the handwritten music score:

"YUB GUB! HOH MEE EECHEE EENEE! YUB GUB!"

Written very low in the voice, heavily accented and repeated many times, this phrase became quite hypnotic. We decided it was a sort of war chant and were therefore most curious as to what could be happening on screen. When we had recorded the piece to John Williams' satisfaction, we were delighted when he said: "Go and have a cup of tea everyone - and when you come back we'll show you the bit of film this fits." On our return, a huge screen had been unrolled and the studio transformed into a viewing theatre. We watched and listened open mouthed as the slowly rhythmic deep bass *"YUB GUB"* etc. had been wound up by the Sound Engineer to a very high pitched, fast and squeaky *"yibgib"* and on screen hundreds of little teddy-bear-like creatures capered about. The film was *Star Wars - The Return of the Jedi* and we were the voices of the EWOKS! We collapsed into helpless laughter as we realised our Turkish accents had been totally useless. At least our Mr 'Know-It-All' had the grace to look (temporarily) embarrassed.

Usually when the composer of a film score conducts the choir and orchestra he is following the screen action on a small monitor by the conductor's podium. A 'time line' moves across the picture, which corresponds with the time markings on the music score, so the music fits the action perfectly. Sometimes the orchestral recording has already been completed and voices are used to overlay the music to provide extra tension or emotion. In these cases, the already recorded track is played through our headphones and the film could be shown on a big screen, which would help us to find the particular vocal colour or intensity they were after. One such occasion was the film *Krull*. A small group of sopranos was booked, and on being handed the music, we found it was written extremely high and very screechy (lots of "EEEEEE's"). Obviously something particularly nasty was happening on screen. AAAArgh! I think that was the nearest I have ever been to experiencing a heart attack, as the scene featured a *monster* tarantula that was being made even more terrifying (if that were possible) by the hideous noises we were being encouraged to make. Fortunately, all my dear colleagues were well aware that I was seriously arachnophobic and made a tight semicircle around the microphone so I could be on the end, almost with my back to the screen and the conductor. The kind girl in the middle surreptitiously relayed the beat. However I don't think for a single minute I was able to pull my weight in that session, for my throat had constricted and I had to keep breathing deeply to control the horrible waves of panic that kept welling up. I have to say that was definitely the *worst* gig of my whole career.

A highly embarrassing moment occurred when film composer Michel Legrand asked John McCarthy to bring 40 singers along to a studio to record a lively chorus in German - 'Let Us Not Divide' from Bach's *St John Passion*. We all sang this lustily, but when invited to watch the playback did not know where to look - the film showed a very saucy, sexy 'soft porn' lesbian romp! Unbelievably, however, the music was actually perfect for the scene.

One of the most beautiful film scores I had the privilege to be involved with was Ennio Morricone's *The Mission*. When we came to providing vocal texture to the haunting melody 'Gabriel's Oboe' everyone was completely entranced and realised this was very special, as it indeed turned out to be.

By complete contrast, the vocalisation required to build the tension and terror in *The Mummy* was really weird, to say the least. It was obvious that this would be one scary film, as during the recording we managed to frighten the wits out of one another without seeing a single frame of film.

Other scary films were *The Omen I and II* and *Final Conflict*. John McCarthy researched the Black Mass from mediaeval documents and transcribed the evil words. The words, together with the fabulous music by Jerry Goldsmith had a tremendous impression on us all. You could really feel the evil. We all felt that we should be carrying a crucifix and a rosary with us throughout the sessions, but fortunately we came through all right with no mishaps.

After several sessions doing the film score for *Clash of the Titans*, Maryetta Midgley and I were asked to stay behind and provide some 'ethereal' backing for a particular scene. We two had been singled out for this as the director wanted a high, atmospheric 'floaty' sound, which suited us both vocally. We worked very hard for the rest of the evening, singing endless top B's, C's and even D's. We certainly felt we had really earned the extra session fee and were rather proud of our achievement. Several months later we both happened to be in London together when we saw that *Clash of the Titans* was being shown in a Leicester Square cinema. We decided to go and hear how our contribution had sounded. The film itself was not really to either of our tastes, but we valiantly sat there, recognising all the choral contributions, waiting for our 'moment'. As the credits rolled we realised, to our immense disappointment that the whole scene must have somehow ended on the cutting room floor.

One film where my solo contribution *didn't* end on the cutting room floor was Ridley Scott's *Legend*. This starred Tim Curry and a young Tom Cruise in his first major film role. We had spent several sessions on a really tuneful score, written by the great Jerry Goldsmith. This reflected beautifully the fairytale nature of the story and I had sung a couple of solo lines during the recordings. Later, back home, I was just sitting down for Sunday lunch when the telephone rang. It was John McCarthy. "Ridley Scott would like you to go to Abbey Road studios and re-record a song. Now!" he said. Naturally, I was in my car and driving towards London within minutes. When I arrived at Abbey Road I was ushered into the control box and introduced to the famous director himself. He was utterly charming, as was Jerry Goldsmith. It turned out that Mia Sara, the actress playing the film's heroine, had pre-recorded a couple of songs but they were not completely happy with the result. They wanted me to lip-synch and over-dub. This involved me listening to the soundtrack through headphones and simultaneously singing in perfect timing and sympathy to Mia's lip movements, demeanour and breathing on screen. It was certainly quite tricky, but after a few takes they were all happy. I was thrilled to recognise my voice on the soundtrack of the film - and I found an Original Sound Track LP in a specialist record store several years later as well.

RECORDING AT ABBEY ROAD

I was fortunate to work for Fred Tomlinson, a very talented singer/arranger who provided musical interludes for many very popular television series, notably *Dad's Army, Only Fools and Horses* and *The Two Ronnies*. If 'local' characters were required to burst into song in any of these programmes, Union rules decreed that professional singers be drafted in to provide, for example, a church congregation or rowdy pub gathering. So it was that when Del Boy and Rodney decided to go carol singing in an *Only Fools and Horses* Christmas Special, half a dozen of us, dressed warmly to combat the 'winter chill', gathered in a street near the Ealing Studios (which was to double as a more salubrious area near Peckham) for the day. Unfortunately, although it was the Christmas episode, filming took place in August, and typically for an English summer, it poured with rain all day. The intention was to use a special technique whereby day could appear night, but unfortunately this was not feasible when raining. An anticipated quick, one hour morning filming session dragged on and on. In the event, we all spent the whole day in a local pub, where our totally inappropriate dress bemused all the regulars. A jolly time was had by all - eating, drinking and playing silly games - until around 9pm there was a break in the weather. We then stumbled out, lustily sang a couple of carols and went home. This was probably the most profitable day of 'not working' I have ever done, as the royalty cheques are still coming in.

One of the most popular sections in each of the episodes of *The Two Ronnies* series was the musical finale, and here Fred excelled, cleverly arranging Ronnie Barker's witty lyrics to fit well known music. Sometimes singers featured 'in vision' (the Ladies Choir, the Hoe Down, etc.) At other times, voices were on a backing track. One of these was the 'Marionettes' sequence. Fred telephoned and said: "Glenys, can you sing *words* on a top 'D'?" Surely it should have been: "Glenys, can you sing a top 'D'?" However, listening to the cassette tape I have of that particular recording, "twinkling toes and tapping feet" comes over loud and clear - so yes, I guess I could.

* * *

In the early 1980's, *Your 100 Best Hymns* was a popular Sunday evening television programme, made by Yorkshire Television. Well known recording artists would take part, singing hymns and religious songs. A small group of Ambrosian Singers, under the banner of The John McCarthy Singers, would travel to the television studios in Leeds for a week, every couple of months, to appear as backing singers and sing our own 'solo spot', recording half a dozen episodes at a time. We were uniformly dressed in cream; the gents in slacks and open necked shirts and ladies in a sort of flowing 'one size fits all' dress. Standing on plinths ranged around the studio, I am sure our resemblance to angels was not entirely coincidental. It was around this time that I was going through a divorce. Despite that fact that this was extremely amicable, it triggered in me a latent sort of rebellion that, sadly, manifested itself in my rather eccentric appearance. I was in my thirties, so I think 'elderly punkette' is probably the best (and kindest) way to describe this regrettable lapse in good taste. Easily dealt with when I turned up at the Leeds Studio for another batch of recordings, were the boiler suit, bizarre eye make-up and black nail polish, but the poor designer and make-up girl blanched at the sight of the burgundy and shocking pink stripey hair...

* * *

Having cut my teeth in the D'Oyly Carte Opera Company, I have since taken part in many concerts, recordings and videos featuring the Gilbert and Sullivan operettas. One such was a series of films featuring 'names' such as Keith Michell, William Conrad ('Cannon'), Frankie Howerd, and Vincent Price as a 'surprise' star in one of the leading roles. A very astute and exacting American businesswoman, Judith de Paul, who would arrive on set each morning in a mink coat and dark glasses, produced the series. The choristers swiftly dubbed her "Cruella de Vil". Even now, some thirty years later, Equity is still trying to claim royalties that really *should* have been awarded to those who participated in these films. George Walker, a very successful businessman, well known however for his shady dealings and dubious enterprises, originally bankrolled the whole series. One day, George visited the set during the filming of *The Mikado*. He arrived accompanied by an entourage of sidekicks, all dressed like gangsters in a 'B' movie - sharp suits, 'co-respondent' shoes, dark glasses and camel-hair overcoats slung across very broad shoulders. After a few minutes of listening intently to W.S. Gilbert's witty lyrics, one of the henchmen was overheard to say to George: "Great idea of yours to do opera in English, boss".

SECOND INTERVAL

VICTORIAN BRASS

When the Royal Opera House reopened in 2000 after its major rebuild, a series of Monday Lunchtime Recitals was established. These took place in the Crush Room, which with its red plush seating, gilt mirrors and glittering chandeliers is an incredibly glamorous location for a recital - and proved very popular with both performers and audiences. There could be anything but opera in the recitals, and this concept gave us singers wonderful encouragement to explore a wealth of songs both ancient and modern. My mezzo-soprano colleague Andrea Hazell and I grasped this opportunity with great enthusiasm. We would settle on a 'theme' and then set about discovering lesser known duets and solos, in order to compile what we hoped would prove an interesting programme to present for consideration by the Opera Company management. Our first recital was entitled *On Wings of Song,* a programme of solos and duets which would have been popular as after dinner entertainment in a Victorian drawing room. At the piano was Jennifer Partridge, one of Britain's leading piano accompanists. Our next venture was *Seasons in Song,* self-explanatory and mostly duets; followed by *Sing a Song of Sixpence - Songs of Childhood*, which was a fun programme of nursery rhymes and songs written for children by surprisingly eminent composers including Sir Arthur Bliss and Benjamin Britten. We were joined by a baritone colleague, Jonathan Fisher, for a programme entitled *Lionel Monckton and Friends - the 'Lost' Musicals* - glorious songs, duets and trios from largely forgotten Edwardian musicals such as *Floradora* and *The Geisha*; and then a programme called *Johann Strauss - Anything But Fledermaus,* where we managed to avoid singing *anything* from Strauss' most famous and popular operetta. All these recitals benefited from several further performances in various locations outside of the Royal Opera House, but the one we repeated most often was *On Wings of Song.* Andrea, Jenny and I expanded the original one hour programme to two 50 minute 'halves', kitted ourselves out with Victorian-style costumes and presented the show all over the country at Music Clubs and other suitable venues. We decided that, as we were doing so many *On Wings of Song* concerts, it would be a good idea to make a CD to sell at these performances. This proved to be an extremely good concept and it is very satisfying to have a permanent record of something we are proud of achieving.

ON WINGS OF SONG Publicity shot

We received an invitation to perform a version of the original recital at the Dickens Festival in Rochester. This is a two day event attended by thousands of visitors every year in the run up to Christmas. There we were, ensconced in the imposing Council Chamber in Rochester, together with a very un-Victorian electric keyboard. Our original brief was to play three shows (at 11am, 2 and 4 pm), but our performances were so oversubscribed, with people queuing outside, that we ended up repeating the show at 12 and 3 as well. Ten shows in two days was a real marathon!

On Wings of Song performances were always great fun to do, but one show was particularly memorable. Shortly before Christmas we were at the Finchcocks Piano Museum, a beautiful Georgian manor house in Kent. The setting was ideal; a stunning wood-panelled drawing room accommodated a capacity audience, and Jenny was particularly enjoying playing a wonderful period grand piano. The concert started at 3pm and we were about a third of the way through the first half, when suddenly a terrible cacophony of noise started up. The fire alarm had been activated. Of course, with a full house of members of the public and a building stuffed to the rafters with priceless and irreplaceable musical instruments, this could not be ignored. Ushered out into the very cold and windy car parking area, we all awaited the arrival of the fire brigade. Of course the audience members had managed to put on their coats and scarves, which were mostly on the backs of their chairs, but we were in our Victorian silk finery, and certainly not dressed for a chilly December afternoon. Amazingly, the fire service arrived within minutes - two engines with flashing blue lights and sirens blaring. Jenny, Andrea and I were soon wearing firemens' jackets; Jenny was also sporting a huge pair of firemens' gloves, as she was so worried about her hands getting too cold to continue playing. The cause of the alarm was soon identified; it appeared that some mince pies being warmed for the interval had overheated. The building was checked, declared safe, and we all trooped back into the house to resume the concert. It is quite difficult to regain the atmosphere of a performance after such a dramatic interruption, but we concentrated hard for the next couple of songs and were just about to embark on the pre-interval finale when - oh dear - it all started up again. This time the fire engines were back on the scene even more swiftly, as they had only got as far as the village; so we were soon back in our warm firemens' jackets and milling around in the courtyard with the audience, whilst the building was being given the once over yet again. Someone wisely suggested we should cut our losses and go straight to the interval - at least with the mince pies eaten they would be unlikely to cause any more trouble. The fire crew enjoyed a share of the warm pies, and then decided that it might be a good idea if one engine remained 'on site' for the second half of the concert, just in case... Fortunately we were able to complete the programme without further interruption, but it was particularly reassuring to see the six burly fire fighters squeezed in at the back of the room.

* * *

In another venture, Jenny and I teamed up with James Watson, the principal trumpet of the Royal Opera Orchestra and formed an ensemble called **VOX OTTONE**. Jim had come up with the idea of performing operatic duets with a soprano, with the trumpet 'singing' the other voice. This may sound bizarre but with Jim's sensitive, musical and very vocal style of playing, it really worked. We decided to make a CD recording, again to sell at concerts, and to our great delight the 'master copy' found favour with the record company ASV, and the CD ended up commercially issued on their White Line label. (N.B. copies are still to be found on Amazon to this day). One particular track, the Flower Duet from *Lakmé* by Delibes, has proved to be most popular and this was included on another CD released by ASV of classical themes used in advertising. This duet appeared, heavily featured, in *Perfect Strangers,* a made-for-TV film, but now I realise it must have somehow ended up as a 'library clip' as it was not specifically credited at the end. This assumption gained confirmation when, not long ago, I was watching an episode of *Homes Under the Hammer* on television when I suddenly became aware that it was indisputedly *me* singing on the soundtrack. Unfortunately, ASV was taken over by Sanctuary Records, which in turn was taken over - and everything seems to have disappeared into a black hole. (When I have finished this book, I think my next project should be to track down any royalties, which surely *must* be outstanding...)

As well as being a superb trumpet player, Jim was an extremely talented conductor of brass bands, and he took first the Desford Colliery Band, and then Black Dyke Mills Band, to win the National Brass Band Championships. It was a great thrill for me to be in the 'players' box' at the Royal Albert Hall on each of these winning occasions. I enjoyed performing as guest soloist on several occasions with both these world-class bands. Songs from my normal concert repertoire were arranged for brass band, and one of my 'special career moments' was standing on the stage at Huddersfield Town Hall singing with Black Dyke Mills Band during one of their sell-out Christmas concerts. Wonderful memories.

Following their triumph at the Royal Albert Hall, Desford Colliery Band played to a packed house at the de Montfort Hall, Leicester. As a guest artist, I was wearing a specially chosen purple sequin ball gown, which complemented the band's very smart purple livery. My first number was a Nacio Herb Brown song, 'Love is Where You Find It'. This was perfect for making a grand entrance as there is a big brass fanfare at the start, following which the band 'vamps' (repeats the same couple of bars over and over) until the soloist is ready to start singing. I received a rousing introduction: "LADIES AND GENTLEMEN, PLEASE WELCOME etc. etc..." and then the band launched into the fanfare as I strode purposefully onto the stage. I was about two thirds of the way on, by which time the band was vamping away, waiting for me to arrive at the front of the stage and start singing, when - DISASTER!! The stiletto heel of one of my gold 'performing' shoes found what must have been the only crack in the wooden stage floor and became solidly stuck. I could not move. Realising they had been playing the same two bars for a ridiculously long time, some members of the band started to turn in their seats to find out what was happening. I tried desperately to extricate myself from this tricky situation - but the shoe just would not budge. There was nothing for it but to step out of both my shoes and continue my journey onstage. Of course, by now I was six inches shorter, and with swathes of purple sequins falling in pools around my stockinged feet, I padded to the centre of the stage and began to sing. Relieved, the band members launched into the song with gusto and we continued with the performance - but all the time I was singing I could see, out of the corner of my eye, a little pair of gold mules sitting there on the stage. What on earth should I do? My mind was racing; there were two and a half thousand people in the auditorium; I could not pretend nothing had happened - *somebody must have noticed.* Eventually, my final cadenza accomplished, the band rose to a grand crescendo and the song came to an end. When the applause died down, I said to the audience: "Thank you everyone - now I'm sure some of you may have noticed that a funny thing happened to me on my way to the centre of the stage this evening...." I then turned and glared accusingly at the miscreant footwear. At that point Jim, taking stock of the situation, leapt down from the conductor's podium and strode towards the shoes.

Crouching down (he is 6ft 5in), he started tugging away, trying to dislodge the embedded heel. At last, after no little effort on his part, he managed to release it and came back to where I was standing. Gallantly, he knelt down in front of me and I was able to use his shoulder to steady myself as I slipped the shoes back on. Impulsively I said: "Oh, they fit! You'll have to marry me now!" Two thousand four hundred and ninety nine people laughed and applauded - but Jim's lovely wife Julie was distinctly 'unamused'!

ACT 3

THE GARDEN PARTY - GETTING AWAY WITH IT

Scilla Stewart and I met at John Murphy's seaside concerts and quickly became firm friends. Together with another colleague, baritone Roy Gregory, who was also an accomplished pianist as well as being a marvellous singer/performer, we decided to form a group to take advantage of the newly emerging popularity with events planners to hire opera singers to entertain at corporate dinners. We called ourselves **THE GARDEN PARTY** and made it known that we were available for corporate events, fund raising concerts and private parties. We were 'spotted' by Clive Thomas, the Managing Director of an upmarket corporate entertainment company and work came flooding in, particularly for our speciality: 'Music on the Menu' - arias and ensembles performed between the courses of a formal dinner. We devised a programme comprising a short and punchy opening set before the first course, followed by longer (15/20 minute) sets before and after the main course and ending with a rousing half hour finale after coffee. We were invited to perform at some amazing and diverse venues including stately homes, livery halls and 5-star hotels, with clients always on the lookout for more and more unusual and exciting places to impress their guests - the likes of Madam Tussauds, the Bank of England, the Royal Yacht Britannia, the Chelsea Gardener (a *very* posh Garden Centre in the Kings Road) and Harvey Nichols - where we set up our portable keyboard in different departments to entertain Harvey Nicks Platinum Cardholders at a special after-hours Christmas Shopping event. (This proved to be a very expensive evening for me, as our last performance was in the China Department and I fell in love with an expensive 'designer' ceramic meerkat and ended up blowing my whole fee).

THE GARDEN PARTY AT MADAM TUSSAUDS
WITH "DUDLEY MOORE" AT THE PIANO

Some venues provided quite a challenge and we eventually became quite good at making the best of a difficult situation when it was thrown at us. Carpeted rooms with low ceilings presented a hideous acoustic. We learned (by bitter experience) that you *never* work even a <u>small</u> marquee without the benefit of amplification. Some rooms were very odd shapes, resulting in several tables of audience members being out of sight of the piano and so we learned to move around whilst singing in order to try to engage everyone. Long thin rooms were a nightmare, as were inconveniently placed pillars. In the Great Hall at Warwick Castle we sang at a dinner for a large European bank, where the florist had gone completely overboard. A floral extravaganza the size of a large shrub adorned each table. The diners could not even see each other across the table, and for us it was like working in a psychedelic forest.

However, I think the most challenging venue of all was the Post Office Tower. There is *only one* extremely small lift accessing the spectacular revolving restaurant at the top of this iconic building, and security was extremely strict. Therefore everything for the evening (keyboard, costumes and music) had to be transported via this small lift, well before the guests were due to assemble. Once there, we realised it was not going to be an easy night. With the diners sitting at tables on the revolving platform, we had to set up shop on a small static area in the middle, which we shared with the kitchen access. (The kitchen was on the floor below). So, whilst we were singing, the audience we were facing gradually disappeared, as a new table came into view... We performed as many concerted numbers (especially trios and quartets) as possible, with a singer placed strategically in each quadrant of the revolve. That way, we reckoned everyone could see *someone* and hear *something*, but it was extremely distracting at times. Definitely one of our most memorable (but very enjoyable) evenings.

* * *

Audiences could be difficult too. Just because the Chairman of a company may have been an opera buff did not mean that all his guests would be equally entranced by an evening of classical music - although we endeavoured to include mainly the most popular operatic items in the programme. Nevertheless, Scilla and I would get great pleasure from the looks of surprise when we burst, unannounced, into a room with tambourine and castanets as we launched into the gypsy 'Chanson Bohême' from *Carmen.*

In order to maximise our popularity, we began to introduce Show songs into the programmes, if requested. We also devised a 20 minute 'scena' from Andrew Lloyd Webber's musical *Phantom of the Opera,* and performed it semi-staged and in costume. When we included *Phantom* in a programme, Roy was always delighted when the room we were performing in had a chandelier and he got particularly good at organising atmospheric lighting whenever possible.

One wonderful booking was for a corporate with a larger than usual budget and we had great fun putting together a (for us) spectacular show. The theme was 'Piccadilly to Broadway' and we performed scenes and excerpts from several stage musicals, including *Cats*, *Phantom of the Opera* and *My Fair Lady*. I spent many a happy hour trawling charity shops for items to create costumes, but the 'piece de résistance' was being able to hire a replica of the black and white 'Ascot' costume, complete with enormous hat, as worn by Audrey Hepburn in the film version of *My Fair Lady*.

We were given a large enough budget to engage an accompanist (Roy and Scilla usually shared these duties, as well as singing), another male singer, a professional 'sound man' to provide head microphones; and, to top it all, the head of the make-up department at the Royal Opera House came along with wigs, moustaches and his full make-up kit. The face painting and wigs for the *Cats* excerpt were quite stunning. The venue was 'Vinopolis', a huge wine warehouse/emporium near Tower Bridge and the guests, who numbered nearly 200, enjoyed an extensive wine tasting tour before dinner. Naturally, their enthusiasm and appreciation for our performances gave us another fantastic night to remember.

Unfortunately, not all audiences were so appreciative. One disastrous evening found us persuaded (much against our better judgement) to perform during a cocktail reception at the Institute of Contemporary Arts in The Mall. The 200 or so guests had been enjoying the host's extraordinarily generous champagne hospitality for a good hour before the organiser decided it was time for us to start. The deafening roar of hundreds of excited conversations only dipped ever so slightly when we started our programme of popular operatic arias. After a couple of numbers, we decided to concede the battle and spent the next half an hour singing to ourselves - and a few curious people who had drifted over to our corner to find out what the noise was all about.

Over the years we have performed at some really prestigious locations, including castles (Windsor, Warwick, Leeds) and palaces (Blenheim, Whitehall); but, at the other end of the scale, we have also thoroughly enjoyed entertaining at a small 40-cover bistro at the seaside. However, all these performances had one factor in common. When discussing the proceedings during a late night drive home, we always liked to feel reassured that despite any challenges the venue had presented us with, or the disposition of the audience we had been striving to entertain, we had managed to *"GET AWAY WITH IT"!*

LOCATION, LOCATION...

For our first bookings at Blenheim Palace we performed in The Orangery, a glorious conservatory situated on the left hand side as one enters the courtyard of this magnificent building. One of these bookings was for a wedding reception, the bride's father having made a fortune in the bakery business. Known in the trade as 'The Doughnut King', it was really no surprise to see that his daughter's wedding cake was a giant doughnut.

A while later, we were booked again to perform at Blenheim Palace. This time the event was an even grander affair, and the dinner took place in the stunning Reception Hall of this huge stately home. However, imagine our delight when a subsequent invitation to Blenheim found us performing at a small and very exclusive dinner party in an exquisite private drawing room at the heart of the Palace. We really felt we had *arrived*.

Talking of 'arriving' - a very red-faced Scilla joined the rest of the group before a corporate party at The Lanesborough, an extremely up-market 5 star hotel in central London. When booking us, the hotel had offered parking spaces in its underground car park; a welcome 'perk' of which we were delighted to take advantage. Scilla had pulled into the taxi access at the front of the hotel to enquire about the car parking and an enthusiastic bellboy rushed out and *insisted* on valet-parking her car. Unfortunately for Scilla it was just after school half-term holiday and her au pair had been ferrying her youngsters and their pals around to various activities all week. The interior of the car was, to put it mildly, in a bit of a state. When retrieving the vehicle at the end of the evening she was mortified to find her ancient, scruffy, litter-strewn hatchback parked jauntily between two large, shining and immaculate brand new Mercedes saloons.

PRIVATE VIEWS

One of the advantages of being involved in a performance 'after hours' at a venue normally open to the general public, is the opportunity to enjoy an exclusive private viewing of some very special attractions. Among these privileges, we enjoyed the fabulous Fabergé Collection at Luton Hoo, the Tutankhamun artefacts collected by the 5th Earl of Carnarvon at Highclere Castle and the somewhat dubious pleasure of a 'private' trip through the Chamber of Horrors at Madam Tussauds.

On the occasion of our first visit on board the Royal Yacht Britannia (very soon after it had been de-commissioned), whilst the guests dined in the State Dining Room, we were accommodated in what had been Princess Diana's private dressing room - a room which was not on the agenda of the standard 'private tour' of the Yacht. Very prettily decked out with pink floral wallpaper, it was in marked contrast to the somewhat austere decoration of the bedrooms occupied by Her Majesty the Queen and HRH Prince Philip.

However, my particular favourite occurred during a visit to Brocket Hall. Having been assigned a room in which to change, eat and rest in the original servants' hall, the chaps had visited the 'little boys' room'. They came back, eyes shining and insisted that Scilla and I accompany them back to the Gents. With a great deal of trepidation and laughter, Scilla and I stepped into the room. We could not believe our eyes. The high-level cisterns above the w.c's were clear glass and in each one a goldfish appeared to be swimming gaily. On pulling the chain, the goldfish encountered a veritable Niagara, before resuming its watery meander. I would like to think the creatures were made of plastic, but the boys were very convincing in their insistence that they were real.

A FUNNY THING HAPPENED ON THE WAY TO/FROM...

Sometimes the journey to a venue can prove to be even more stressful than the actual gig itself. A motorway traffic hold-up or missed turn on a country lane, can turn a pleasantly anticipated trip into a nightmare. A professional musician has an in-built horror of arriving anywhere late. But on the other hand, the fact that we usually have to travel far and wide to and from our place of work definitely has its compensations. Who could fail to enjoy the heart-stopping first glimpse of the magnificent Chatsworth House, or be thrilled by the sense of excitement when travelling the mile long driveway to Arbury Hall?

Probably the most remote location we travelled to was Ackergill Tower in Caithness, situated in solitary splendour right on the raging north-east Scottish coast, a few miles from John O'Groats. Courtesy of Prestige Promotions, the corporate entertainment company for whom we did a lot of work, we had provided a 'Music on the Menu' opera evening for the directors of a large supermarket chain. The Managing Director was so pleased with our performance that he enquired of Prestige whether we would be prepared to come and sing at a 'small dinner party' he was arranging privately to celebrate a milestone birthday. He offered to fly us up to Scotland, together with two nights' accommodation, all meals *and* a generous fee. This turned out to be the final event of a long weekend of fun and games held at the said Ackergill Tower. Therefore, it was with great excitement that the four of us met up at Heathrow and boarded our commuter plane to Aberdeen. At Aberdeen we transferred to a small sixteen seater plane bound for Inverness. Not the most confident of air travellers and with the planes getting progressively smaller, Roy was most unnerved when completing the final leg of the journey from Inverness to Wick on a *very* small private plane - especially as, by the time we were airborne, quite a gusty wind had set in. Scilla, Adrian and I were somewhat worried that we would be spending most of our time trying to calm Roy down and preparing him for the return journey. However, Ackergill Tower is quite the most romantic, magical place and it quickly wove a spell, calming even the most frightened of flyers. We had a wonderful couple of days' 'holiday' and thoroughly enjoyed singing to the host's select and privileged guests. When it came to the morning of our departure, it had been organised that our return trip would be by road to Inverness to catch the plane to Aberdeen. Although that meant a very early start, the stunning scenery more than made up for the lack of a lie-in. On the two-and-a-half-hour road journey we encountered no other vehicles as we enjoyed the glorious backdrop of the Highlands. However, all peace and calm was shattered on our arrival at Inverness Airport. For some reason, a lady security officer took a sinister interest in Roy, subjecting his luggage to the most comprehensive of searches. She even took out his cufflinks and minutely examined them. We later learned that this official had been 'tipped off' that we were musicians - and had obviously jumped to far more interesting conclusions than we warranted.

Even further afield, The Garden Party travelled to Geneva and Amsterdam for engagements. In Amsterdam the dinner took place in Oude Kerk - an iconic church of cathedral proportions, and the oldest building in Amsterdam. A taxi took us from our hotel to the venue to do the sound check and then, with a couple of hours to kill before the performance, we decided to explore the surrounding area. Imagine our surprise to find the church is located in the very centre of the Amsterdam red light district! This made for a very interesting stroll back to the hotel after the show, too.

* * *

The Sultan of Brunei owns a very lavish 'summer residence' in the Buckinghamshire countryside, and every July/August the Princess and the ladies of her court come over to the UK to escape the Brunei heat and indulge in some retail therapy. Daily they are driven up to central London to Harrods and Selfridges - and other diversions, such as theatre visits are organised. At the end of one particular stay, a celebration dinner was arranged and Clive (the Managing Director of Prestige Promotions) was approached to provide a musical entertainment: "some ladies to entertain the ladies". The group had attended a performance of *Phantom of the Opera* in London during their visit and so Clive asked if Scilla and I could provide a programme that included several songs from this particular show. We initially had a slight problem trying to convince the organisers that, in order to do the show justice, it was imperative that we had a male performer as well. We explained that neither Scilla nor I would make a convincing Phantom - and the best-known duet 'All I Ask of You' just does not sound right with two female voices. Eventually they agreed, and we were delighted to be able to invite Roy to join us.

The dinner was to take place in a beautifully decorated marquee in the extensive grounds of the property. When we arrived to set up our keyboard, the Sultan's electrician was horrified when he saw the state of our extension lead (which had seen considerable service over the years) and by the time we came to do the show we were delighted to find that we had acquired a new, heavy duty lead, with the Sultan's compliments. (It is still in use today - always referred to as 'The Sultan's Cable'). We were shown into a magnificent conservatory, complete with fountains, waterfall and a grotto, and were plied with all manner of food and soft drinks, whilst waiting until we were required to perform. It was quite the most glamorous 'dressing room' we have ever experienced. When they were ready for our performance we were taken back to the marquee and were somewhat taken aback to find that the room was definitively segregated, with all the ladies sitting round tables on one side and a few men on the other side. The ladies were dressed in the most wonderful array of colours, with enough glitter and sparkle to make a drag queen jealous. After we had finished singing, the men all suddenly disappeared and the room was swiftly prepared for a disco, complete with dance floor and lighting. Back in our glamorous conservatory/dressing room, a member of the Household came to thank us and mentioned that the ladies would be delighted if Scilla and I would consider joining them "for a dance". Casting a quizzical eye towards Roy (for we realised he would not have been included in this invitation), we were delighted when he said that, as he had been so well looked after and the evening was warm, he would be perfectly content to wait in the car listening to the radio until we were ready to leave. Thus it was that Scilla and I, although reasonably smartly dressed but certainly not in 'party' clothes, spent the next hour bopping to Middle-Eastern chart hits with some very exquisite rainbow-coloured butterflies. When we felt Roy had been patient enough, we were escorted back to join him at the car - at which point the organiser thanked us all again profusely and handed over a plain white envelope containing a very generous cash tip. Definitely an unexpected bonus!

As a bizarre postscript to this memorable evening - we asked the organiser: "Which of the ladies was the Princess?" The reply was certainly unexpected. "Oh, the Princess died several years ago, but her Household still carries on the tradition of spending the hot summer months away from Brunei, just as they did when she was alive."

...AND WHEN WE GOT THERE

The Great Room at the five star Grosvenor House Hotel in Park Lane, London, provided us with two very different, yet equally memorable, evenings. The Great Room is reputed to be Europe's largest banqueting hall and can seat over 2000 diners. The first occasion was a grand celebration dinner for the Caravan Club of Great Britain, and Scilla, Roy and I were booked to provide a 15 minute 'opera slot' before the speeches. With Roy at the piano, Scilla and I burst on to the stage area and launched into our first number, 'Chanson Bohême' from *Carmen*. For us, this also involves a lot of dancing and movement as, playing the castanets and a tambourine, we build the dance to its wild conclusion. After our final Gypsy flourish we then moved to stand still together in the centre of the stage ready to sing the 'Flower Duet' from *Lakmé*. It was only then, and with a shock, that we both became aware of the half-a-dozen enormous film screens positioned all around the room. They had been blank during our sound check - but now, with cameras trained directly on us, there we were, twenty feet high, in close-up and glorious Technicolor. Two *very* sharp intakes of breath later and with tummy muscles tensed to a near spasm, we self-consciously continued with our programme. The cameras and screens had been set up because the space was so huge, and they wanted every guest at the dinner to be able to see a short film later in the proceedings. For us, it was a most unnerving experience.

ON STAGE AT GROSVENOR HOUSE

A while later, the Events Coordinator from the Grosvenor House telephoned and invited Scilla and me to perform "one aria at a select dinner party." With Scilla accompanying me, I elected to sing 'Song to the Moon' from Dvorak's *Rusalka*, my favourite operatic aria. We arrived at the hotel to learn that this dinner was to celebrate the fact that Marriott Hotels had acquired the Grosvenor House as their flagship hotel in London and a dozen of the top executives from both organisations were dining. Imagine our astonishment when we learned we would again be performing in the Great Room. This time the room had been dressed in a spectacular fashion, with black drapes and twinkly pea-lights, creating a magical starlit effect. The rest of the huge space was in total darkness, with just one dining table, set for twelve, in the centre. It was dressed with beautiful candelabra and exquisite flower arrangements. Clever lighting gave the surreal effect of a dining table 'floating' under a vast canopy of stars. A grand piano had been set up, but hidden under the cover of darkness. Scilla and I crept out into the blackness and lurked behind a convenient pillar until a discreet lighting cue signalled it was time for us to approach the piano. Thank goodness we could just about make out the white keys of the piano - or we would surely have bumped into the instrument. Then, to the diners' surprise a spotlight suddenly lit us, and we performed the aria. The acoustic in that cavernous space was amazing (I had no microphone) and it was just like singing in a cathedral. I think that must have been my favourite time singing my favourite aria. Then, all too soon, it was over and we were plunged back into complete darkness. It took us a few minutes for our eyes to readjust, before we carefully and stealthily negotiated our way towards the starlit backdrop and back down to earth...

* * *

The Garden Party quartet was booked to entertain at a welcome dinner, preceding a week of high level conferences and site visits for senior executives of Maersk, the international shipping firm, held in an exclusive country club set in the beautiful Northumberland countryside. The twenty-four delegates had flown in from every corner of the world - and it had even taken us all day to make our way to the remote venue. The offer of overnight accommodation and use of all the Club's facilities meant we were really looking forward to a paid 'mini-break'. Our first two short sets (after the starter and after the main course) went down extremely well and our small, yet exclusive, audience proved to be both enthusiastic and appreciative. Our final set was due to follow the 'welcome' speeches after the dessert course; so we changed costumes and waited for the organiser to call on us to perform our finale. After what had seemed an interminably long time, Adrian went to find out where they had got to in the proceedings. To his consternation he found the dining room deserted - with the tables cleared and chairs stacked. Eventually he managed to locate the event organiser in the empty bar, bidding goodnight to two remaining delegates. "Oh dear", she said, "everyone was so tired after the day's travelling, and with the prospect of a 6.30am helicopter pickup to take them to the first site visit, they all decided to retire to bed. I totally forgot you were prepared to sing some more." She came along to our room to apologise to us all. "But we saved our best numbers for the last set!" we wailed. However, she managed to assure us that everyone was delighted and very satisfied with our contribution to the evening - and after a conciliatory nightcap in the bar we, too, had an early night.

One job that *DID* finish, despite almost overwhelming odds, was an 'Opera in the Park' fund-raiser for the Fitzwilliam Hunt in Cambridgeshire. The venue was idyllic. We were to perform on the steps of a magnificent Orangery set in the extensive parkland grounds of Milton Park, with the audience invited to picnic prior to the performance on a vast lawned area leading down to the edge of a beautiful lake. A professional sound and lighting company had set up a sound system and floodlit the stage area. Over 1000 people had purchased entrance tickets in advance, with many more expected to turn up on the gate. Throughout our afternoon sound check, clouds were gathering ominously but although it remained overcast, it was dry as the gates opened at 5.30pm and the picnickers began arriving. We returned to our Green Room to change into our finery and be fitted with radio mikes for the evening show. Just before 7.30pm, a Land Rover arrived to ferry us up to the Orangery and as we got in - Scilla and I in our fullest, most extravagant ball gowns - the first drops of rain began to fall. By the time we reached the performance area, this had developed into a real cloudburst. There was no way we could traverse the pathway to the Orangery without getting drenched so we huddled together in the Land Rover, hoping it would blow over. After 20 minutes we realised that the downpour was probably set in for the evening and a 'Continue or Cancel' situation had arisen. After a very brief discussion we came to a unanimous decision - if the audience were prepared to brave the elements, we would not let them down. The show would go ahead. Someone had wisely moved our keyboard under cover into the Orangery and hastily erected a couple of temporary gazebos on the steps, over part of the performing area. We made a mad dash from the vehicle towards the (relative) cover of the awnings. As we ran into view, a huge cheer came from the picnickers. We had not reckoned with the stoicism of the hunting fraternity. Not one person had gone home. There they all sat - huddled under huge golfing umbrellas, tarpaulins and makeshift tents. How could we have wimpily disappointed them? The only downside was that for many in the audience, their hands were fully occupied holding umbrellas, and so enthusiastic umbrella waving took the place of applause after each number. Fortunately the rain did ease after half an hour or so and we were able to venture down the steps from under our protective awning. This inadvertently provided the greatest laugh of the evening - as Scilla sang the 'Habanera', from *Carmen*, she danced energetically along the path at the base of the steps, castanets clacking. Suddenly, out from the huddled groups in the audience dashed a small terrier - which proceeded to chase Scilla across the lawn, yapping exuberantly. The umbrellas went wild!

More uninvited and unexpected attention from wildlife took place at a dinner for Barclays Bank in the Great Conservatory at Syon Park. This elegant, plant-filled glasshouse proved a very special venue for a corporate dinner - and it provided the most amazing acoustic in which to sing. The popular 'Flower Duet' from *Lakmé* by Delibes has a coda at the end and when it is performed on stage, Lakmé and her companion Malika walk off into the wings and vocalise the familiar tune. Normally Scilla and I will finish the duet just before the coda but, if the venue has a suitable 'offstage' exit, we would carry on through to the 'official' end of the duet to create a magical ending (we hope). Syon was indeed eminently suitable for this extension of the duet, so as Roy continued playing the accompanying chords, Scilla and I walked slowly to the nearest exit, deftly opened the glass door and stepped out into the starlit night. Leaving the door open, we proceeded a few steps down the gravel pathway and prepared to vocalise the final phrase. About six feet from the doorway, a peacock - in full display, blocked our path. As we drew breath to sing, he joined in - very, very loudly! The audience could not believe its ears - thunderous applause for us both and our unexpected accompanist greeted our return to the room.

We always try to utilise features of the venue in which we are performing to enhance the 'staging' of items. For example, some large spaces have internal balconies that can be perfect for creating an atmospheric 'Barcarole'; or a room with several entrances and exits can be most useful for staging the Papageno/Papagena duet. Heavy window curtains are great for hiding behind, either to make a surprise entrance (*Pagliacci* or *Faust*) or to divide the performing area (*Rigoletto* quartet). Traditionally, Mimi and Rodolfo should sing the last couple of phrases of the love duet from *La Bohême* offstage, so Adrian and I always tried to ensure that by the end of the duet we were near a doorway. At Hagley Hall, the guests were dining in an exquisite yellow-silk-lined reception room and our duet from *La Bohême* was on the programme. As we reached the climax of this most romantic of duets, Adrian gently took my hand and, gazing lovingly at me, opened a door and led me into a broom cupboard, closing the door firmly behind us. In total darkness, we crashed into a bucket and mop and knocked over a small step-ladder. We tried hard to stifle our giggles, but I have to admit that it was not the best top 'C' either of us had ever sung. Sheepishly, we emerged from our cubby hole - and then noticed that the double doors leading into the reception hallway were much further down the room...

* * *

Apsley House is the former home of the Duke of Wellington. Situated at Hyde Park Corner, it rejoices in the address 'Number One, London' and is one of the most exclusive venues for a corporate event. Only the most extravagant of hosts treat their guests to an evening of fine dining and entertainment there. Security was extremely tight - definitely the most strict we had ever previously encountered anywhere. There seemed to be security guards stationed at every doorway, to escort us to and from our changing rooms and the Waterloo Gallery where we were to perform. After we had sung our first set, we repaired to the State Dining Room where places had been laid for us to eat. Our 'minders' stood guard while we waited for our meal to be served. In the centre of the huge table (it must have seated twenty-four) was an amazing centrepiece. Fashioned from silver, from what I can remember it depicted several horses being ridden into battle. It was quite the most over-the-top extravaganza I had ever seen. We all gasped as we saw it and as we sat down Roy instinctively reached out to touch one of the animals. Immediately someone screamed: "don't touch it!" and poor Roy nearly jumped out of his skin. Apparently the whole arrangement was priceless and was security alarmed - as were most of the artefacts and paintings in the building. Suitably chastened we sat down to eat; quite terrified to move or touch anything, in case we set off one of the many alarms in the building.

One unusually warm summer's evening found Scilla, Roy, Keith and I performing for a tour group of Americans, who were dining at Goodwood House in the South Downs. The group, about thirty of them, sat at a single table in the magnificent Ballroom of this stately home. Our assigned dressing room was the Card Room, an exquisite circular room leading directly off the Ballroom, which has on display the Goodwood Sèvres porcelain collection. We had set up 'camp' there and had thoroughly enjoyed performing to jolly and appreciative guests. However, after our final set, the group was scheduled to have a short AGM and 'discussion time' over coffee and liqueurs. As we had finished our contribution to the evening, we were anxious to get going back to London, but we had no idea how long they would linger over the petits fours. Unfortunately, the only exit from our 'green room' opened straight into the Ballroom and naturally we did not want to disturb the guests. In any case, due to the warmth of the weather we were all very casually dressed (Keith was in shorts and sandals.) Then Keith had a brainwave: "we're on the ground floor - we could climb out of the window!" With the alarming alarms at Apsley House still fresh in our minds, it was with much trepidation that we allowed Keith to attempt to raise the sash window. It opened! He then, very slowly and carefully, climbed backwards over the windowsill and dropped down onto the flowerbed below the window. As he straightened up and made to retrieve his suit bag we all heard a vigorous round of applause. Turning round, to his horror, the group of Americans were standing about ten yards away, watching intently with barely concealed amusement. In the few minutes it had taken us to hatch and execute our 'escape plan', they had finished their coffee and exited Goodwood House - just in time to see Keith emerging, bottom first, from the ground floor window right by where their coach was parked. A very red-faced Keith bowed solemnly and then proceeded to pick up his suit bag before sauntering off to find his car.

FOOD, GLORIOUS FOOD

Without doubt, the best 'perk' of a Garden Party outing was the opportunity to "sing for our supper". After choosing a fabulous location, company bosses and wealthy private individuals would then source the very best chefs to provide elaborate culinary delights with which to impress their clients and friends. That would only leave the entertainment to complete a memorable evening - and so naturally The Garden Party would be booked! Scilla and I were well prepared for the initial telephone conversation - after discussing the basics such as availability, type of programme and fee, the client usually enquired whether we preferred to eat before or after the performance - or - horrors - would we like a tray of sandwiches? Our stock answer: "Why don't we make it easy for you and your caterers - we'll have what your guests are having", invariably facilitated the desired result. Thus it was that over the years we have sampled some of the most amazing meals, cooked by some very famous chefs (Prue Leith, Anton Mosiman and Michel Roux to name but a few).

The first time we performed at Mosimans, we were fortunate enough to enjoy our meal in the Chef's Dining Room. It was an exquisite room, with glass panels on three sides and was set at first floor height overlooking the busy kitchen of this Michelin starred restaurant. We all found it totally mesmerising to watch skilled chefs at work - and it was with no little reluctance that we had to tear ourselves away from the fascinating scene to perform our sets between the courses. The food itself was simply wonderful, in both flavour and presentation. Served with a stunning 'collage' for dessert, we gazed at our plates in awe. "I'd like to hang this on my wall," Roy remarked wistfully, before he gave in to temptation and demolished the work of art with gusto.

One year, the CEO of a well known pharmaceutical company decided to indulge a fantasy and set about commissioning a series of small corporate dinners to take place in nearly all the Cambridge Colleges. Held over a three month period, so all invited guests were able to choose a convenient date to attend , each evening took exactly the same format - the same wines, the same menu and the same entertainment. We found ourselves regularly driving up and down the M11, but with a different venue to find in Cambridge each time. Each College had its own special atmosphere and catering staff. We began to award marks out of ten for the meals, in particular the crème brulée, which was the dessert of choice. The waiting staff could never quite understand the level of excitement among the singers caused by the serving of a crème brulée. (In case you are interested, the overall winner was St John's.)

A particularly favoured invitation was one to perform on the Royal Yacht Britannia for a Carols by Candlelight evening - not only is this iconic venue exquisitely decorated with Christmas trees, candles and fairy lights, but also a decidedly gourmet meal is always served and we are given a home made Christmas pudding on disembarking.

WITH SCILLA ON THE STAIRCASE ON BOARD THE ROYAL YACHT BRITANNIA

People regularly ask how on earth we can do justice to a three course meal - *and sing*. All I can say is that, faced with the prospect of a beautifully prepared, cooked and served dinner - which to all intents and purposes is part of our fee - you just make sure that you *do* enjoy it. It can be hard, believe me, but after years of training I can assure you *it can be done*.

However, one evening proved far more difficult than anticipated. The venue was again Mosiman's Dining Club in Belgravia. Scilla and I had thoroughly enjoyed our dinner - especially Anton Mosiman's signature bread and butter pudding, which perfectly rounded off the delicious meal. Alarm bells should have rung as we changed into another dress prior to embarking on our final set. Nevertheless, we both ignored the warning signs of the struggle to do up the zips and made our way down to the dining room. We had elected to start this set of songs with the duet from Bellini's *Norma* - 'Mira o Norma'. This showy duet, mainly sung in thirds between the High Priestess Norma and the handmaid Adalgisa, starts in a heavy operatic style and ends with a very fast and furious cabaletta (lots of notes, ending on a high 'C'). As Adalgisa opens the number, Scilla started singing the first verse. I thought her singing sounded a little laboured, but did not fully realise the extent of the problem until it was my turn to answer her with the second verse. It was horrendous. My dress was so tight I could not take a decent breath and it was an enormous effort to make any sound at all. It felt as if every mouthful I had eaten was hanging on my larynx. As the duet progressed, it got more and more difficult and we both had to work harder and harder to keep going. As we eventually launched into the cabaletta, with all its vocal runs and leaps, we instinctively clutched each other's hands for support - willing each other to carry on and finish the marathon. At last it was over and with great relief we waddled off so the tenor could take the stage. Later, our distinctly unsympathetic pianist enjoyed a good gloat. "Well, at least that will teach you not to eat so much before you sing that duet in future", he laughed. "Not at all", we chorused in unison: "It's taught us to never put *that* duet so late in the programme next time...."

A COMMERCIAL BREAK

With the increasing popularity of the use of classical music in films, television and advertising, we have often joked to our audience that we could do a whole evening just singing the adverts.   If we were performing for a large company or corporation, we endeavoured to personalise their evening by incorporating their own particular 'theme tune' at a suitable point in the proceedings.   For example, we included a much appreciated quartet version of 'Va Pensiero' from Verdi's *Nabucco* for a Concorde reunion dinner.   If the company did not have a specific musical calling card, then we enjoyed coming up with an item easily recognisable as complementing their product or service.   A couple of our more inspired offerings were 'The Flower (Flour) Duet' for Homepride Bakeries and, when we entertained the bosses of Powergen, who were then sponsoring the weather forecast on television, I sang 'One Fine Day' from *Madama Butterfly*.   We were at Brocket Hall, singing at a dinner for executives of mobile telephone company Nokia, when our baritone Rodney produced a master stroke.   He was singing Figaro's aria 'Largo al Factotum' from *The Barber of Seville* and somehow managed to get his mobile phone in his pocket to ring loudly with the unmistakable Nokia ring-tone in the middle of the aria.   He then proceeded to 'answer' the call and sing a large part of the aria as a telephone conversation.   As you can imagine, this went down a treat with the guests - more satisfied customers.

One evening, Scilla and I were singing the *Lakmé* duet, probably best known to the general public as the 'British Airways' duet. As we commenced the second verse, Scilla (and she says it was a total impulse) started to wave her arms as though flying.   To this day, we still marvel at how in tune we were with one another - by the end of the duet we were instinctively doing the actions of a Flight Attendant's safety briefing, in time to the music. This had our audience in fits of laughter - we had a hit on our hands. We spent a few minutes refining the actions before the next outing and quickly found this to be one of our most popular and requested items. So much so that when British Airways won a coveted Travel Award, to be presented at a prestigious award ceremony at the Hilton Hotel in Park Lane, Scilla and I were asked to perform this duet *a capella* (without accompaniment) as a surprise just before Sir Richard Attenborough handed over the trophy. The organisers had really hoped that we would be able to dress up as BA cabin crew but at the last minute a 'security issue' put a stop to that. In the end we hid behind a pillar in matching concert dresses, with Scilla humming the start notes (thank heavens she has perfect pitch), ready to leap out in front of a startled Sir Richard to give musical accompaniment (with appropriate actions) as the BA bigwig walked up to the stage to collect the award.

REHEARSAL?? WHAT REHEARSAL??

In order to keep our shows and ourselves 'fresh' we were always learning new items to include in performances - or we would accommodate particular requests for specific bookings. We would often use spare time at venues before the guests arrived to musically rehearse and choreograph concerted numbers for future use, but sometimes we could slot a solo item directly into a performance with a minimum of rehearsal. For example, I had taken it upon myself to learn Musetta's Waltz Song from *La Bohême* and decided to give it a first public airing during a dinner at Hanbury Manor. Scilla was delighted, as she had been nagging me to learn this song for ages. I had sourced a copy of the aria in E flat, which is a semitone lower than the original in the score, as this sat very well in my voice. A semitone down does not sound too much of an advantage but, believe me, it means all the difference when singing on a full stomach. This aria would prove most useful as the first item after the main course at one of our 'gourmet' dinners. The introduction to the aria is two bars followed by three 'bell notes' played on the piano, which gives the singer the key to launch into the song. As this was the first time Scilla and I would have performed this together, we were fortunate to have the opportunity to go through the song a couple of times before the dinner. I was feeling rather pleased with myself as the run-through went without mishap and I agreed with Scilla that it was a good aria for me. After the main course, Scilla entered the room first, sat at the piano and played the three 'bell notes' as I made my entrance. Afterwards, I professed that I was sadly disappointed with my performance. The rehearsal had gone so well, but in the event it was such hard work. Scilla just nodded sagely and ventured that as it was the first time in public, perhaps the nerves had kicked in and made it feel difficult. Many, many months later Scilla confessed that she had, in fact, sat down at the piano and automatically played the starting notes in the original - higher - key. It was only when she looked up at the music in front of her that she realised - too late - what had happened. She then had to continue playing the aria in the key she had started me in, transposing up as the song progressed. She said she was too embarrassed to admit this at the time - but it proved to me that one should always be nice to one's accompanist - they have the power to make or break a performance.

If things can go haywire after a careful rehearsal, it is surely tempting fate to dispense with a rehearsal altogether....

Scilla was accompanist at a regular afternoon concert at the De la Warr Pavilion, Bexhill on Sea and I was often booked as a guest artist to do a 15/20 minute solo spot, along with a baritone. As these bookings depended on our current availability, we guest artists often did not get to meet each other until an hour or so before the show, when we would quickly decide if we also had any mutual duets that we could perform after a very brief rehearsal. One afternoon, Bob the baritone was delayed on the journey down to Bexhill and we had no time for a duet run-through. However, he asked me: "Do you do the Papageno/Papagena duet from *The Magic Flute*?" Fortunately I did, as I had recently learned it for an audition to cover the role at the Royal Opera. We decided that we both knew the duet well enough to take a chance without a rehearsal. When it came to the performance, Scilla spoke to the audience to set the scene. In her introduction she explained that Papageno was half man, half bird and in this duet, which comes at the end of the opera, he finally gets to meet his true love Papagena, who is half girl, half bird. They excitedly plan to raise a whole nestful of chicks and live happily ever after. Scilla then started to play the introductory bars and in order to 'act out' the duet, Bob entered from the wings, singing: "Pa-Pa-Pa..." Entering from the opposite side of the stage, I answered him: "Pa-Pa-Pa..." With short bird-like steps we travelled towards each other, "Pa-Pa-Pa-Pa..." until at last we met in the centre of the stage. "Caught! At last no more I'll lose thee", sang Bob as he caught my hand. My heart stopped - Oh NO! He's singing it in *ENGLISH*! I had learned it in German. Trying to disguise my panic, I had to think quickly. I had an answering phrase, so I repeated the words Bob had just sung. A slight flicker of surprise crossed Bob's face, but he carried on: "You'll be mine to your last feather..." I doggedly followed, repeating and paraphrasing each line he sang. Fortunately I had been well coached on the piece and I knew it securely enough musically to continue singing *something* - either parroting Bob, or making up a vague translation of the German when I could, until after what seemed to be an interminable duet, we finished on a final flourish of "Pa-Pa-Pa's" and fluttered bird-like off into the wings together. Once there I collapsed in a heap, not knowing whether to laugh or cry. "That was a bit of an odd translation you had there - what edition does it come from?" asked Bob innocently, before laughing heartily when I had confessed my predicament. After that, I always made sure I established what language we would be singing in as soon as a duet appeared on a proposed programme - and to make doubly sure, I learned the English text of the most popular duets in my repertoire.

THIRD INTERVAL

HERE COMES THE BRIDE...

To sing at a wedding can be an absolute joy - but some have more joy than others, and often the bride and groom are totally unaware of this...

The Choir of the Carmelite Priory was booked to sing a full Latin Nuptial Mass at the Kensington church, at a wedding where the bride came from a large Caribbean family. We had been singing a selection of suitable religious pieces from the organ loft at the back of the church prior to the bride's arrival, when our director, John McCarthy, received the 'go ahead' that she had arrived. (This techno-wizardry comprised a light bulb screwed to the side of the organ). We immediately launched into the full Bridal Chorus from Wagner's *Lohengrin* ('Here Comes the Bride'). A large, flamboyantly dressed lady on the arm of a scrawny little man, proceeded to walk slowly and majestically down the aisle below us, greeting the wedding guests warmly and occasionally stopping to hug and kiss a favoured guest. We glanced at each other in mild surprise as she was certainly a little more mature than we expected but - hey - she was taking her time, which meant that we were able to sing the whole chorus without the all too often embarrassment of the bride reaching the altar within the first few bars. In fact we finished the chorus a few seconds before she came to a halt at the top of the aisle, so we swiftly handed in our music to conductor John McCarthy. We were preparing to start the Walford Davies 'God Be In My Head' when one of the mezzos frantically indicated that on reaching the altar she had immediately turned left, swept into the front pew and sat down together with her escort. It was the bride's mother, not the bride! Bruce, the organist, had already played the opening chord for God Be In My Head, so he had to extemporise to get us smoothly back into the right key while John hurriedly dished out the *Lohengrin* copies again. We then struck up with the Bridal Chorus for the second time as the correct bridal party walked down the aisle.

* * *

Usually the bride and bridegroom are only too pleased to take advice as to what I should sing during the signing of the register, but sometimes they request a specific song. One such time was when the bride wanted me to sing 'O Mio Babbino Caro' from Puccini's *Gianni Schicchi*. I did express my surprise at this, as it is the aria where a daughter attempts to blackmail her father into letting her marry a young man he considers unsuitable by threatening to throw herself into a river. Nevertheless, the bride was adamant. "It's the theme from the film *A Room With A View*", she insisted. "Anyway, this is not going to be a *conventional* wedding by any means." She was not exaggerating. On the day, as everyone stood and turned for a first glimpse of the bride, there was an audible gasp from the assembled congregation. The bride wafted down the aisle in clouds of tulle. *Black* tulle...

* * *

Occasionally the Choir of the Carmelite Priory was booked to sing at a wedding away from the Kensington church. One such time was a very 'posh' winter wedding in deepest Oxfordshire. The village church was stunningly beautiful and exquisitely decorated with lit candles for the late afternoon ceremony. John McCarthy informed us that the bride had been most specific about the music she wanted for both before and during the service. As well as a selection from the standard repertoire of choral wedding pieces, she wanted a choral arrangement of the Agnus Dei from Samuel Barber's *Adagio for Strings*, together with Allegri's *Miserere Mei* to be included in the music sung in the 15 minutes or so before she arrived at the church. Neither of these pieces was in our usual repertoire of wedding music, so we were going to have to concentrate hard to get them right. The last item scheduled was the Allegri composition to coincide with her arrival at the church door. The plan was that she could hear it whilst having photographs taken before beginning her walk down the aisle. *Miserere Mei* is a truly ethereal piece - a haunting setting of the twenty verses of Psalm 51 - quasi plainsong in style, with a soprano/treble solo voice repeating a phrase which soars to a high 'C' over the rest of the choir at the end of each alternate verse. Debbie had bravely elected to sing the high solo line and, twenty minutes before the ceremony was due to start, we began the programme with the Barber piece. As we neared the end of the Allegri we realised that the bridal party had not yet arrived at the church, so it was decided to begin the whole programme again - and cut to the final item as soon as she turned up. Twenty minutes later she was still nowhere to be seen, so we started back to the beginning again. After a full hour, and three complete repeats of the programme, the candles were burning very low and the congregation was understandably getting rather restless - chatting and fidgeting. As for the choir; well, by then we had certainly mastered the difficult Barber piece and poor Debbie, having sung over twenty top C's, had definitely had enough. To our immense relief, we heard a slight commotion outside the church door and guessed/hoped that the bride had eventually arrived, so John McCarthy decided to repeat the Miserere 'on a loop' whilst we waited for her to at last enter the church. It then became obvious that the bride had managed to engage the slowest, most pernickety of photographers on the planet. To give Debbie a break, first Lynda and then I took over the solo line in turns as we repeated the piece *three* more times! Eventually, a total of 43 top C's and an hour and twenty minutes later than anticipated, we were mightily relieved to launch into the Bridal March from Wagner's *Lohengrin* - with rather more gusto than usual. On the way home, vocally exhausted and rather hoarse, we all decided that despite our enhanced 'out of town' fee, the bridal party certainly had their money's worth that day.

* * *

John McCarthy telephoned me one day to say that Maryetta had unfortunately found herself to be 'double booked'; could I possibly fill in for her as soloist at a wedding in Ealing. Thrilled to be considered as Maryetta's 'understudy', I accepted with alacrity. It was then I discovered that maybe there had been a method in Maryetta's unprecedented lapse in diary management. This wedding would appear to be a case where the bride was totally unable to make a decision as to what music to choose to be included in the service, so had elected to try to fit in as many solos as possible. I was to start with Salvete Christi (a vocal solo arranged to the tune of *Finlandia* by Sibelius) as soon as the bride arrived at the altar. This was followed, at various times during the service, by Ave Maria (Schubert); Laudate Dominum (Mozart); Panis Angelicus (Cesar Franck); Alleluia (Mozart) and finally, Rejoice Greatly (from Handel's *Messiah*). A friend of the bride was to play the clarinet in a duet with me in the Panis Angelicus and then she was giving a solo rendition of Jesu, Joy of Man's Desiring (Bach). However, when we arrived at the church prior to the service to rehearse with the organist, she found that the organ was a quarter-tone sharp, making it impossible for the clarinet and organ to play in tune together, so the organist asked me to sing the Bach as well. In all, I sang a total of *seven* lengthy items that afternoon. What a marathon! I am sure the wedding guests must have wondered if they had wandered into a recital rather than a marriage ceremony when I kept popping up with yet another vocal contribution every few minutes or so.

* * *

Picture the scene - a wedding ceremony in a beautiful old church in a very picturesque Buckinghamshire village. The bride and groom had requested that I sing Mozart's Laudate Dominum during the signing of the register. A few weeks before the service, the organist got in touch to say that the organ had started misbehaving, occasionally becoming unreliable in the volume department, and although he felt it would be fine for the hymns, he was concerned about playing for the solo. Would I mind if he accompanied me on the church piano? Naturally I agreed that it would be no problem at all. When it came to the time for the happy couple to repair to the vestry to sign the register, I stepped out in front of the altar and the organist made his way from the organ and sat down at the small upright piano temporarily positioned in front of the chancel rail. The Laudate Dominum has a rather long introduction and I was happily surveying the faces - and hats - in the congregation when, out of the corner of my eye, I suddenly became aware of what seemed a rather strange occurrence... The organist's arms appeared to be getting longer and longer. It took several more bars of music before I realised what was happening. The piano had been wheeled into place along the stone flagstones - *but had not been anchored!* The floor had a distinct slope and the piano, whilst being played, was slowly moving away from the pianist. The poor man was struggling to keep in contact with the retreating instrument, attempting to shuffle his chair towards the keyboard as he valiantly tried to do Mozart justice. With mounting horror I realised that in about thirty seconds or so I would have to start singing. Suddenly there was a slight kerfuffle in the choir stalls behind me: fortunately a sharp-eyed baritone in the church choir had realised what was happening. He sprang into action, clambering past and over several indignant soprano choir members, who were completely unaware of the crisis. When he reached the chancel rail, he leaned over the instrument, immediately

113

above the organist (who found himself forced to crouch over the keys to continue playing) and hung onto the piano lid, which effectively arrested its imminent escape. How I got through that aria without dissolving into hysterics I will never know. All the time I was singing I had visions of the piano, with accompanist in hot pursuit, disappearing down the aisle! When I recall that incident, even today, I can still see the gentleman in the third pew who had resorted to stuffing his hankie in his mouth to stop himself laughing aloud.

BIRTHDAY BLOOPERS

Many years ago, I was booked to perform a 'singing telegram' at a 70th birthday party held in a large country house in Kent. It was a real cloak and dagger affair and I was under very strict instructions to keep the surprise element to maximum effect. My accompanist was travelling with his keyboard from North London, and we had arranged to turn up before the guests and go into hiding until everyone had arrived and the party was in full swing. I duly arrived in good time and presented myself at the back door. With much giggling and exaggerated secrecy, one of the catering staff ushered me into a small room off the kitchen that was to be my changing/hiding room. This proved to be a sort of pantry-cum-garden store containing shelves stacked with kilner jars, various brooms and a couple of dilapidated garden chairs. Oh the glamour! Still, a contract is a contract, so I set about changing into the sequinned ball gown in which I was to surprise the guests with a birthday song. I could hear a lot of activity in the kitchen and adjacent corridor as staff and guests mingled, and soon the party was well under way. I settled myself into the less rickety of the two chairs and waited for my summons. And waited. And waited. I started to feel rather uneasy as I had been there for such a long time. I also had a real dilemma - I was hardly inconspicuously dressed and if I ventured out, it would be just my luck for the hostess to see me, ruining the surprise. With mounting panic, I realised I was trapped. Oh for a mobile phone! Unfortunately, such a lifesaver had yet to be invented. What I could not know was that the pianist, John, was caught in stationary traffic due to a road accident in the Dartford Tunnel, with no way of letting anyone know. When he eventually arrived - on his own - there was apparently great consternation until a waitress suddenly remembered shutting someone in a cupboard some four hours earlier...

On another occasion, a very wealthy socialite had invited Scilla and me to sing at a birthday party she had arranged for her husband at the Dorchester Hotel on Park Lane. They were staying in a penthouse suite and she very generously suggested that we use this accommodation to get ready for our performance. Thrilled to have such a luxurious 'dressing room', we took great pains with our hair, make-up and eyelashes. The phone rang to summon our presence - so we dived into the bathroom for a quick 'mirror check' and we were poised and ready to go. Scilla grabbed her pump action hairspray and gave both our hairdos a generous going over. Too late, she realised that on leaving home she had packed the wrong refillable bottle and this one was full of water. We ended up singing the Venetian 'Barcarole' looking as though we had both just fallen OUT of the gondola.

* * *

One client booked us to perform at a huge party to celebrate his wedding anniversary on a large, luxurious party boat that sailed on the Thames from Maidenhead. We chose our programme carefully - taking into account a request for lots of romantic items - and it appeared to be enjoyed by all guests, in particular the anniversary love-birds. Imagine our surprise when, less than three months later, we were booked for a repeat performance. Same boat, same programme, virtually the same guests. The only difference was that this time Mr B had a new girlfriend! In the few intervening weeks, he had managed to obtain a 'quickie' divorce from the first Mrs B and this time was celebrating his engagement.

YOU HUM IT...

One important lesson I have learned over the years is never *ever* to believe someone who blithely says: "Oh yes, there is a lovely piano and it was tuned only last week..."

One man's 'recently tuned' instrument is another man's performance nightmare. To this end, the Garden Party has now purchased a top of the range electric keyboard, usually transported to a gig by car, unless the piano at the venue is known and trusted. More often than not, said keyboard remains in the car park but any inconvenience caused by its transportation is more than justified by the sense of security its presence gives us. However, despite taking all reasonable precautions, over the years I have still encountered some PIANO DISASTERS.

Some years ago, Roy and I were booked to provide the after dinner entertainment at an Association of Estate Agents annual dinner at a hotel in Ealing, West London. As was quite normal for this type of gig, if it was reasonably local and we were not scheduled to appear until after the meal, we would 'check out' the venue late in the afternoon then return around nine ready to perform. At this venue a temporary stage had been erected at one end of the function room and a DJ was setting up all his disco equipment at one end of what looked to be a decidedly dodgy construction. Standing next to the stage was a rather battered upright piano. Roy expressed a little concern that the piano was "on its last legs", but felt that if we left well alone we could probably get away with it. However, after we had left the venue in search of a fish and chip supper, someone had the bright idea of getting the piano 'out of the way', so this also found itself manhandled onto the somewhat rickety raised area. Roy was not best pleased, on entering the room to take up his place at the instrument, to find that not only had it been moved onto the 'stage', it had also been positioned so that he had his back to the audience and therefore he had limited contact with me. Still, he did not make a fuss and just started playing the introduction to my first song. He says that he then realised that the piano had a distinct list to it as the weight of all the disco equipment was causing the stage to slope quite dramatically and he was really concerned that the piano would topple over. As I was in front of him, I was totally unaware of his predicament as he resolutely played on, but the piano had decided that the trauma of being manoeuvred onto the platform was just one indignity too far. Suddenly, with a very loud crash, the sustaining pedal parted company from the main body of the piano and rolled down the sloping stage, landing at my feet just as I finished the song. Poor Roy was beside himself!

* * *

A lovely Scottish lady, who lived locally, had asked me if I would come and sing at a dinner party. "I have a beautiful wee piano which belonged to my father", she informed me. When my accompanist, Iris, and I arrived at her home (having practised the programme with Iris playing her own grand piano) we were in for a shock. It was indeed an exquisite little instrument, but the emphasis was squarely on the 'little'. Her father had been a naval captain and the piano was a 'ship's piano' with a folding keyboard, designed to fit into small spaces on board ship and it comprised only five octaves, compared to the normal seven and a half. I think I must have given rather a distracted performance as I watched, fascinated, as Iris's hands constantly waved around in thin air, reaching for piano keys that were not there.

* * *

When it comes to pianos, even the best laid plans can be thwarted. As a member of a quartet which regularly performed at Grimsdyke (W. S. Gilbert's country house), we were booked to sing a Gilbert and Sullivan programme between dinner courses for a group of American tourists, who were staying and dining at the Cumberland Hotel near Marble Arch. I decided that I would be very thorough and telephoned the hotel to ascertain that they had a piano we could use. I spoke to a very helpful receptionist. "Oh yes," she said, "we have a lovely grand piano here in the first floor reception area. I can see it from my desk here. It is positioned just outside the function suite you are scheduled to use, so we can easily roll it into the room when you arrive." Suitably assured, I arranged to meet Scilla, the pianist, downstairs in the street level reception area only an hour before the clients were due to arrive for their meal. As we ascended the flight of stairs to the first floor main reception we could hear the sound of a piano being played - Scilla nodded approvingly. Reaching the top of the stairs, as we looked for the piano to see who was playing so beautifully - the smiles were instantly wiped off our faces. *There was no one sitting at the keyboard.* Scilla advanced towards the instrument and with great trepidation, lifted the lid. Straight away, her worst fears were confirmed - it was empty, apart from a cassette deck playing recorded piano music. This lovely white baby grand piano was a dummy; an interior designer's prop. Then it hit us - we were due to entertain a coach load of overseas visitors in less than an hour's time and we had *no piano*. Action stations! I rushed off to find the tour organiser, to sweet talk and attempt to delay our performance, whilst Scilla telephoned home where her husband was just putting her small daughter to bed. He obviously registered the panic in her voice and, to his immense credit, swung into instantaneous action. Small daughter was strapped into her car seat; he loaded the children's Casio keyboard into the car and immediately left to do battle with rush hour traffic from south to central London. By the time the poor, stressed man arrived at the hotel the guests were already having the dessert course and we were rehashing our proposed programme for the umpteenth time. We set the keyboard on a table, where alas, it looked as ridiculous as it sounded. Then, to our understandable relief, it emerged that the Americans had arrived in the UK early that very morning, immediately embarking on a gruelling full-day 'Sights of London, including Windsor Castle' tour. They were practically falling asleep into the Summer Pudding - and scheduled to leave for Edinburgh at dawn the next day. No one was at all upset when we offered to sing just a couple of songs and let them get off to their beds (least of all us).

* * *

A prestigious corporate dinner found us driving up to the wonderful Highclere Castle (later to achieve fame as 'Downton Abbey'). The boss of the corporate entertainment company which was organising the evening had been told that there was a 'marvellous' Broadwood grand piano in situ, so there was no need to hire one. We all arrived together, were very impressed by the superb reception rooms, and were delighted when informed that although the library was not usually available for dining, special dispensation had been granted for our event. Finally, we were introduced to the piano. Indeed a magnificent instrument, it would definitely enhance our performance, apart from one small problem. It was not *in* the library but in an anteroom, *next door* to the library. Over the years, we have acquired a great deal of experience in repositioning pianos gently and efficiently, so without further ado we set about moving this monster a few feet through the double doors into the room where we were scheduled to perform. Suddenly we were confronted by an extremely officious gentleman who told us in no uncertain terms: "that piano must NOT on any account be moved!" Our predicament was of no concern to him and our arguments and entreaties fell on deaf ears. He was adamant - the piano was going nowhere. For us, this heralded a performance disaster - both the baritone and mezzo-soprano in the group were extremely accomplished pianists and shared the accompaniment duties. Naturally this involved singing in the operatic quartets and some trios 'from the keyboard'. Obviously these items would have to be dropped from the programme as not one person in our audience could see the piano - and for the remaining arias and duets, the singers' movements would have to be curtailed drastically. We usually varied our performing position in the room when entertaining an audience seated at tables, in order to engage with as many people as possible during an evening. The situation we found ourselves in at Highclere meant that we all had to sing everything whilst hovering in the doorway, in order at least to maintain a vestige of contact with the accompanist, who had to abandon any contemplation of musical dynamics and simply bash away as loudly as possible. It was a far from ideal situation; our original programme had been blown to smithereens and we had to quickly cobble together a mix of the more static items in our repertoire which would hopefully come across as both interesting and entertaining. This eventually proved to be one of our most stressful and taxing evenings and matters were not improved when, as we were packing up to leave, the gentleman who had been the sole cause of our problems announced: "well done everyone - if I had known you were as good as that I would have let you move the piano......." Grrrrr!!!!

* * *

"Carols by Candlelight" was a very popular Christmas entertainment, whereby we would sing Christmas themed music to diners in iconic candlelit venues. These included Middle Temple, Whitehall Palace, and Colleges at both Oxford and Cambridge Universities. The tenor, baritone and I had arrived in good time at St John's College, Cambridge and we were waiting for Scilla, our mezzo to join us. She was very late and we were becoming worried, when she telephoned (on her new ' brick' of a mobile phone) to say that she was stuck on the northbound M11 as there had been a nasty accident just ahead of her and the road had been closed so that an Air Ambulance could attend the scene. Although relieved that she was okay and at least pointing in the right direction, we became anxious again as time passed and the guests began arriving. It was then that we realised that the hired piano from Marksons had not turned up either. I phoned Scilla to pass on this news. "Oh dear", she said, "there's a Marksons van three vehicles ahead of me - I bet it's in there..." (It was).

* * *

One weekend, as luck would have it, we had a job on both the Friday and Saturday evenings. Friday found us performing at an 'Opera in the Park' outdoor extravaganza in aid of the Fitzwilliam Hunt in Peterborough, and on the Saturday we were booked for a fund-raising Opera Gala for the Duke's Barn Trust at Chatsworth House, Derbyshire. Our Clavinova keyboard was perfect for the outdoor gig as it could be hooked up to the sound system, but as the Chatsworth opera evening was a very posh black tie affair attended by the Duke of Devonshire himself, the organisers had hired a grand piano for the occasion. We had all decided to stay overnight in a hotel near the Leicestershire venue and then make our way onwards to Derbyshire, where we were welcomed with tea and cake at the Duke's Barn Outdoor Activity Centre, a couple of miles from the magnificent Chatsworth House. We were unable to gain access to the House until after it was closed to visitors, so when we arrived a little after 5.30pm a scene of frantic activity greeted us; caterers unloading; people moving tables and chairs; flowers arriving; everyone rushing to get the room ready for the Champagne Reception at 7pm. Having already performed a very similar programme the previous evening we had no real need to rehearse but, all the same, Scilla pointed out that she could not see a piano anywhere. The young lady in charge had a moment's panic but was greatly relieved when she found the acknowledged piano hire order in her folder. However, as time marched on we thought it wise to suggest she telephone the hire company to check on the piano's progress. The raised area at the top end of the room was perfect for a stage, but if the piano did not arrive soon it would be highly awkward to manoeuvre it through the dining tables that were rapidly being set and dressed. Her face was white when she came off the phone - there was no piano on its way. The company had *forgotten* to send it out. How on earth could anyone *forget* to deliver a grand piano to one of the greatest stately homes in the country? The poor girl was on the verge of tears. However - all was not lost - we quickly dashed to the car park and retrieved the trusty Clavinova from Scilla's car. On the raised stage it certainly looked absolutely ridiculous in the grand and opulent surroundings - but it saved the day. You can imagine the huge cheer that went up when, in my 'welcome' remarks I explained the situation and then, with a flourish, gestured towards the instrument, saying: "and fortunately - here is a spare we found in the boot of the car!"

ACT 4

COVENT GARDEN -
FUN AT THE FACTORY

I started singing with the Royal Opera extra chorus in the early 1980's when John McCarthy became Chorus Director. Several years and three Chorus Masters later I was thrilled to join the permanent 'regular' Chorus - and so the Royal Opera House, Covent Garden became my home for 25 years. The rehearsal schedule for the Royal Opera Chorus is pretty relentless. Each week, two or three opera performances take place on the main stage in the evening (alternating with ballet performances by the Royal Ballet). An opera in its final stages of rehearsal (with either piano or orchestral accompaniment) occupies the stage in the mornings, and up to two other operas are in production in one of the two main rehearsal spaces within the building. At the same time the Chorus is preparing musically (and memorising) maybe five other operas for future productions. Before the first production rehearsal it is required that all chorus music should be committed to memory. Costume fittings, shoe fittings and wig fittings have also to be accommodated. No wonder the House is known affectionately as 'The Factory'.

We usually sing operas in their original languages - Italian, German, French, Russian, English and Czech. (We have language coaches to help with the pronunciation.) When I first joined the company there was a relatively large contingent of Welsh men in the Gents chorus, known collectively as the 'Tafia'. One year we were, for reasons beyond our ken, performing the opera *Don Carlos* in its Italian version on the stage, yet at the same time we were making a studio sound recording of this opera in French. When people grumbled and questioned the wisdom of this endeavour, a member of the Music Staff remarked: "I don't know what you are getting all het up about - the 'Tafia' is singing both versions in Welsh anyway."

On many occasions, either at the behest of the composer or, funnily enough, because a director has drawn a blank on how to incorporate around fifty or so extra bodies into a particular scene, the chorus sings in the wings - known as an 'Off-Stage Chorus'. Surprisingly often this can occur towards the end of an opera, as in *Aida* and *La Traviata*. This leads to the 'perk' of being able to get out of costume before curtain down - with an additional bonus of being able to leave the theatre promptly and thus get into the lift at Covent Garden tube station before the West End audiences get there. Some bright spark noted that there were many of these unseen (but nevertheless well-known) choral contributions - and whilst John McCarthy was the Chorus Master it was mooted that we should make a CD of popular Off-Stage choruses. John said he would look into getting this idea sponsored by Tesco - with the disc entitled "Carrier Bag Choruses", as he was invariably faced with a group of singers with coats, hats and gloves on, all clutching plastic carrier bags of shopping, ready for the 'off'.

The days are long gone when singers were required to do no more than stand stock still on stage and simply *sing*. All performers (and that most definitely includes choristers) are expected to act and dance as well. The Royal Opera chorus are well known (within the ranks of other professional opera companies) as being particularly (annoyingly?) willing - and indeed 'gung-ho' when it comes to realising opera directors' sometimes more extravagant flights of fancy. We have it on good authority that the chorus of another 'A' list European house (naming no names...) has proved extremely difficult when a production had transferred from Covent Garden - and we tended to regard reciprocal stagings as rather static and boring. Stopping short of actual ballet (we have a very competent group of Opera Ballet dancers who are brought in should the production demand it), we have over the years learned to waltz, minuet, line dance and disco-bop with the best of them. One particularly exciting extramural activity occurred in *Re in Ascolta* (Berio). All choristers who did not suffer from vertigo could take part in a 'flying' sequence. We were fitted with harnesses under our costumes and, to the audience's astonishment, suddenly rose up towards the flies where we dangled at varying heights whilst singing a choral episode in this modern opera.

Another minor diversion, guaranteed to provide a welcome distraction to our day, is the Fire Drill. Although we are always aware that this is going to happen, it can be scheduled to occur at any time of the day, and in any sort of weather. The ruling is that everyone has to evacuate the building *immediately*, whatever he or she is doing or wearing. On several occasions a Fire Drill has interrupted a stage rehearsal and we have all poured into the Covent Garden Piazza dressed in the most outlandish costumes, much to the bemusement of the many foreign tourists wandering around. The trouble is that most of them think we are just another group of 'Street Theatre' actors and so they automatically tend to form a semicircle around us and wait patiently for us to perform some tricks...

CORSETS, WIMPLES ......AND RAGS

Whilst it would be very wrong of me to complain about the wonderful array of costumes a chorister is privileged to wear (particularly in 'period' shows) we have to accept that we are very much at the mercy of the Designer - and sometimes it is very difficult to comprehend what is behind a particularly outlandish idea. Two that immediately spring to mind are *Cherubin* (Massenet) and *Damnation of Faust* (Berlioz). One of several costumes in *Cherubin* required all the choristers (both male and female) to sport blue faces and full size French baguettes on their heads, and *in the same show*, another had us wearing shocking pink faces and moustaches. The Crowe's Cremine (stage make-up remover) did sterling work during that run.

CHERUBIN

As for *Damnation of Faust* - well, I am so glad I have a photograph to show that all the ladies wore huge false breasts, wellington boots and a raffia wig - giving the appearance of a troupe of pornographic Worzel Gummidges leaping about!

ANNE OSBORNE and ANDREA HAZELL
DAMNATION OF FAUST

Several shows have had the chorus ladies dressed as men - both 'doublet and hose' or full formal evening attire, either DJ or Tails. This would entail the wearing of uncomfortable (for many) 'bust flatteners', but it was amazing how successful this transformation could be - especially if the ensemble is finished off with a glued-on moustache.

One fascinating fact I learned early on is that when designing a 'period' costume, it is crucial to get the foundations exactly right. We wear boned costumes, or corsets, to achieve the correct body shape for the garment to look right. A Victorian corset is made and fastened in an entirely different way from an Edwardian corset.

A boned bodice should *not* be worn with a bra, (a garment we modern ladies find very hard to dispense with) but we had a great deal of fun when doing a production of *Falstaff,* set in the 1950's. The designer sourced authentic post-war brassières (rather amusingly substantial and 'pointy') which we had to wear under her scrupulously correct evening gowns. Due to the success of *La Traviata,* designed by Bob Crowley, the Company decided to replicate all the costumes, to remain at Covent Garden when hiring out the production to foreign opera houses. At the fittings, there was consternation when it became obvious that the replica ball gowns just did not look quite as stunning as the originals. Then an astute seamstress realised that the bodices had been cut and boned using an 18th century template instead of the required 19th century one. The dressmakers had to remake all the garments before they were deemed satisfactory. When fastened with laces, costumes can accommodate the vagaries of weight loss/gain, even pregnancy, and we have professional dressers to help us in to and out of the dresses. Our dressers all become very adept at lacing or hooking corsets and bodices (they need to be particularly strong to manage to get us into some of the more restricting underpinnings!) They are also under strict instructions to police any incidents where choristers may 'accidentally' forget to put on the required corset (usually following an over-indulgent lunch). At the end of a show wherein all the ladies are laced into costumes it would be usual to find an 'undressing chain' winding around the room, with all the girls pulling at the laces of the one in front, in order to expedite the journey home.

An interesting fact about theatrical costumes is that zips should *never* be used on the professional stage. A 'shop bought' garment, acquired for a contemporary production, has the zips removed and replaced with hooks and eyes or buttons. These are, of course, much fiddlier to deal with but, unlike a zip, in an emergency are much easier to repair. Velcro is another useful tool in the costume department, particularly for quick changes. Sometimes a director needs a complete change of costume to take place within a severely restricted time - maybe only half a page of music. For a soloist this can be sorted with relative ease but if there are, say, sixty choristers to organise it can become a logistical nightmare. Addressed with military precision, tables and chairs are laid out meticulously with the appropriate clothing in exact positions, plus mirrors and tissues in the case of a change of wig and/or make-up. The first attempt at a fast mass quick change is always a complete shambles, and it never ceases to amaze us when it all comes together after a couple of run-throughs.

However, the most common outfit for a lady chorister would be that for either a peasant or a nun. Peasants would range from the picturesque - dirndl skirts, embroidered pinnies and pigtails, to the downright unsavoury - a bundle of grey 'rags' which, although actually perfectly clean, had been cleverly 'broken down' and made to look as though they had been slept in, on the floor of a pig sty, for years! As for nuns, we have been posh nuns, poor nuns and all nuns in between - from modern nuns wearing gabardine raincoats to those sporting headgear resembling ships in full sail.

Some more exotic outfits included belly dancers (in *Die Frau Ohne Schatten*), complete with stick-on navel jewels and clip-on nose rings; and probably the most wonderful - the authentic Japanese Geisha costumes worn by Butterfly's Friends in *Madama Butterfly*. These six gorgeous hand-painted silk kimonos were authentic down to the last detail including the several layers of undergarments, the massive hand-tied obi, and the split-toed socks (tabi) to accommodate wearing the 'geta' (shoes that were a cross between flip-flops and clogs). Wearing these took some getting used to and our progress to and from the stage was very slow indeed. This was one time when there was absolutely *no* chance of getting to the head of the queue for coffee during a break in rehearsals.

The wardrobe department employed a lovely Japanese dresser to help us don these costumes and to ensure we put everything on in the correct order. What with the enormous wig and the special make up, which included soaping out our eyebrows and our faces being covered by a thick layer of chalky white face paint, it really did take twice as long to get ready for our appearance on stage than the whole scene actually lasted.

BUTTERFLY'S FRIENDS

Most disappointing was the time when we learned that the iconic Italian fashion designer Giorgio Armani had agreed to design the costumes for a new production of *Cosi fan Tutte*. The excitement when a full rail of 'designer' trouser suits was wheeled into the wardrobe department swiftly evaporated and turned to consternation when it was discovered that Signor Armani did not 'do' larger than a size 12 - hardly appropriate when dealing with the, ahem, well padded opera singer.... Cue some seriously creative alterations on the part of the wardrobe seamstresses who, it has to be said, definitely saved the day.

WARDROBE MALFUNCTIONS

A horror that haunts every performer is euphemistically known as a Wardrobe Malfunction. To discover on stage, too late, that you are missing a vital part of your costume; that you are the *only* one wearing a red mask when everyone else is in a white one; or you forgot to change from your Act 1 boots into your Act 2 ballet pumps, is the stuff of nightmares. Moreover, a wire coat hanger inadvertently attached to the train of your mediaeval gown is only marginally less embarrassing than a brassière. The more cringe-worthy your predicament, the more vicarious pleasure can be derived from it by your unsympathetic colleagues. Unfortunately, some disasters are self-administered. The ladies sitting in the dressing room will never forget when poor Anna Cooper decided to give herself a manicure whilst waiting for our call for the finale at the end of a long evening. She inadvertently spilled some nail polish remover onto her lap, and we watched in absolute horror as the liquid slowly melted a huge hole in the synthetic fabric of her dress, just as our summons to the stage came over the tannoy.

* * *

If a chorister plays a specific character (either by wearing a distinctive costume, or by a bit of 'business' that is important to the smooth running of the production) then a 'cover' chorister is usually appointed in case of unexpected absence from a show. In the opera *Cherubin*, five ladies of the chorus played 'Manolas'. Their costumes were most exotic - strapless bodices were fashioned from black latex rubber, individually moulded to fit each lady, and the full length gathered skirts were made from electric blue heavy duty suedette; the sort of fabric usually used to make car seat covers, or sofas. They were required to walk across the stage, holding a chocolate cream éclair high in the air in each hand (do not ask), with which to tempt five gentlemen of the chorus. I had to cover all five ladies and, of course, the inevitable happened. On the morning of the General (final dress rehearsal) one of the 'Manolas' called in sick - I was on. As the show was technically still in rehearsal the wardrobe department had not had time to make costumes for the understudies, so we had to make do with the only costume available. Unfortunately, the indisposed Beth was far more generously proportioned than I was and, at best, the rubber top fitted where it touched. However, masters of invention, the dressers got to work and with the help of a well-stuffed strapless "Rawhide" bra (rounds 'em up and heads 'em out!) and a roll of heavy-duty black 'gaffer' tape borrowed from the stage crew, they made a pretty good job of fitting the bustier. The skirt, alas, was an even trickier matter. It was at least an inch too long and far too big around the waist. Eventually three large nappy pins secured the overlap and I was ready to hit the stage. I strode on, arms aloft, clutching my chocolate éclairs and had traversed about two thirds of the way across the stage towards my appointed gentleman, when disaster struck. I trod heavily on the too-long front hem of the skirt and the nappy pins gave way. The heavy skirt immediately fell like a stone to the ground. My immediate instinct was to bend down to pick it up - and to free up a hand, I stuffed one éclair unceremoniously into my mouth. I then discovered that the skirt was far too cumbersome to deal with single-handed, so in went the other éclair and I scuttled off, mortified, into the opposite wings. The delicious éclairs did go a long way to compensate for my embarrassment, but having been denied his greatly anticipated chocolate treat that morning, my 'partner' was none too pleased. Fortunately, a costume made to my own measurements was available by the first night - and subsequent appearances went without a hitch.

UNDERSTUDY 'MANOLA' - *CHERUBIN*

* * *

One day, a young American mezzo-soprano came over to play the title role in *Carmen*. An extremely attractive *voluptuous* lady she was, too. The gents in the chorus thought that all their birthdays had come at once; as it turned out, she was just as interested in *them* as they were in *her*. One young man in particular caught her fancy and she flirted outrageously with him throughout the rehearsal period. It came to the General rehearsal, when the order of the day is: full costume, wigs and make-up. In order to comply with this edict, the young man as a soldier had to sport an extremely large, luxuriantly bushy moustache. Carmen came bounding onto the stage before singing the Habanera. She made a beeline for her favoured soldier and clutched him to her ample bosom. She eventually let him up for air, but unfortunately his moustache had transferred itself to her décolletage and she had to sing the whole of the aria with a *very* hairy chest.

IT WILL BE ALRIGHT ON THE NIGHT (OR WILL IT?)

As a purveyor of dreams, the theatre relies heavily on its sets and special effects to achieve the magic needed to satisfy an audience's imagination. Those of us on stage are, of necessity, fully aware of the nuts and bolts that go into making a scene worthy of spontaneous audience applause - nonetheless we are all very thrilled when we hear that response. Some sets are incredibly complicated and take a lot of getting used to, leading to an unusually fraught rehearsal period. One of the most substantial sets we ever had to work with was in the opera *The Greek Passion* (Martinu). A complex representation of a Greek village tumbling down a hillside filled the whole of the stage area, from front to back and right up into the flies. Steps and lanes twisted and turned like a maze - and woe betide anyone who took a wrong turning. If you happened to arrive at the wrong dead end, there was nothing you could do but turn round and resentfully trudge back up the very steep way you had just come down.

Other sets were breathtakingly difficult to negotiate and control. One in particular, a set for *The Flying Dutchman*, understandably had only one run of performances. A vast mobile stage moved on hydraulics, up and down and round and round (sometimes both at the same time). Members of the chorus were constantly required to negotiate their way onto the moving stage area as it changed position to create another aspect of the ship or shore. Other choristers were crouched below the platform as it swung round. It was absolutely terrifying for all concerned. I remember that my final position on the stage towards the end of the show was standing motionless in a corner at the back. However, by the time the last chords of the opera were being played I was standing on the *front* corner of the stage, which was jutting out over the orchestra pit, and I ended up within a couple of feet of the astonished occupant of seat A8 in the front row of the Orchestra Stalls. It was most nerve-wracking to try and keep one's balance as the stage moved round and I used to practise by standing unsupported on the notoriously 'boneshaker' Metropolitan Tube on the way in to rehearsals. The technical brilliance required to operate such an amazingly complicated set was such that this was the only show I ever recall at the Opera House where the stage crew took a curtain call at the end.

* * *

Sometimes it is only the smallest of technical hiccups that can cause major problems and/or embarrassment. In the Act 1 party scene in *La Traviata*, a footman wheels on a life-sized 'ice sculpture' of a naked lady. By jumping up onto the central banquette and imitating the pose, Violetta confirms that *she* indeed had been the model for it. This is a cue for a shower of glitter to fall from above, which contrives to add even more glamour to the proceedings. One evening, the filtering mechanism which distributes the glitter evenly across the stage area did not operate, resulting in the whole sack of one inch square shiny gold sequins being suddenly dumped, unceremoniously and directly onto the posing Violetta. We could only look on in horror as, to give her her due, Violetta reacted to this disaster with remarkable aplomb. After the initial shock, with a delicate toss of her head she shook the worst of the glitter from her immaculate coiffure, dusted down the front of her ball gown and carried on partying. However, it was with relief we noted that in subsequent performances she took up her Ice Sculpture pose slightly towards the side of the stage.

* * *

Great fun was to be had in one scene of the rarely performed Verdi opera *Il Due Foscari*. The designer had the chorus in pairs, in mini 'gondolas' supposedly sailing across the stage. These craft resembled the trolleys fashioned from orange boxes and discarded pram wheels so popular with youngsters before the advent of skateboards and video games. Just big enough to accommodate two people, they were open at the bottom and ran on four small wheels. Crouched on the seating planks across the 'boat', one of the occupants was required to 'scoot' furiously backwards to make it move, whilst the other tried to steer. Oh, and we were to sing a Barcarole "drifting across the water" type chorus at the same time... I expect this looked quite effective from the Stalls and even the Grand Tier, but I imagine those looking down from the Amphitheatre seats would have had quite a different impression! We regularly seemed to come off the stage after this scene helpless with barely suppressed laughter.

* * *

Sometimes ideas that seem so good on paper turn out to be disastrous in application. The set designer of a rather avant garde production of *Fidelio* wanted the whole of the last scene to be lit from beneath a frosted glass floor. This looked amazing, but then the director wanted the entire chorus, barefoot and dressed uniformly in cream woollen shifts, to sit and/or lie on the floor throughout the duration of this scene. As it progressed, the lights heated the floor to an alarming degree, and it soon became obvious that we were in danger of being boiled alive on a giant hotplate.

* * *

A design idea that did look beautiful was in a production of *Cosi fan Tutte*; the scene where the set undergoes a transformation into an exotic wedding venue. During the entr'acte music, a giant red silk covering already spread over the stage is raised slowly by means of ropes and pulleys from above, to form a beautiful billowing red silk Bedouin tent. At the same time, a trapdoor opens and the chorus would appear from beneath the stage (known as the 'Mezzanine') laden with items to decorate the tent ready for the approaching nuptials.

We would then stand and serenade the bride and groom. To fit in with the overall theme of the show, the half a dozen chorus ladies (Cosi is always a 'small chorus opera') are dressed in flowing black silk burkhas, with only hands, feet and eyes showing. Together with another colleague, it was my job to enter first - each of us carrying an oversize 'terracotta' pot. Fortunately they weighed very little as they were cleverly made of papier mache, but the pots themselves were well over three feet tall and contained some gigantic blooms, making them very unwieldy indeed. Below stage, our cargo was loaded into our arms with great precision, and we then had to ensure that we did not step on the front hem of our costume as we climbed the stairs, virtually blind and with no arm free to steady ourselves. On the exact music cue ("Flowerpot Men Go!" from a gleeful Stage Manager) I would set off on my tortuous journey up the flight of steps (actually little more than a glorified ladder) closely followed by fellow choristers similarly laden with large cushions, rugs and small tables. It was always a great relief to step from our hole onto the stage and to set the pots down in their required positions. However on one occasion, as I neared the top of the stairs, I realised something was seriously wrong. The red silk had not lifted! Conscious of the fact that my eleven colleagues were so close behind - all concentrating hard on getting onto the stage without wobbling, tripping or dropping anything, I ploughed ahead and pushed my way into the yards and yards of billowing red silk, manfully clutching my giant floral decoration to my panicking chest, closely followed by several equally alarmed pals. From the audience's point of view it must have looked like rats trying to escape a flour bag! Eventually - very, very late - the silk flew into the air and we were able to scuttle around placing our items, which this time we had to do whilst actually singing our bridal chorus. Fortunately, the burkhas hid our embarrassed red faces most efficiently.

IN THE SWIM

With the advent of increasingly advanced technology, many set designers have been attracted to the idea of incorporating a water 'feature' into the concept of a production. Both *Madama Butterfly* and *Katya Kabanova* have had water on stage, either flowing, or falling as rain. In one production of *Eugene Onegin*, the Ladies Chorus warbled the 'Blackberry Picking' chorus whilst splashing about in a small river, dominating the scene. I am not sure how the visuals matched up with the translation of the libretto displayed by the surtitles on that occasion - but maybe there are some water-grown soft fruit in Russia?

* * *

In an updated *Les Huguenots* (Meyerbeer), one scene was set around a large swimming pool, which was like a giant paddling pool containing about a foot of sparkling blue water. There was a lot of consternation at the first costume fittings for this show, when it emerged that the ladies were required to wear swimsuits whilst disporting themselves in and around the pool. Half the ladies chorus immediately went on crash diets and the other half demanded stylish beach 'cover-ups' to disguise less than bikini-fit bodies. Both proved good moves as the Press, unsurprisingly, had a field day and half page photographs of this scene appeared in all national newspapers. However, we did not make Page 3 of *The Sun*! During one performance, a member of the audience became so incensed (excited?) by the amount of flesh on display that he attempted to climb over the rail surrounding the Stalls Circle to gain access to the stage, shouting his disapproval. One of the theatre ushers, Ivel, became the hero of the evening by manhandling him to the ground and promptly ejecting him from the auditorium. The performance then continued uninterrupted.

* * *

The show where water played the greatest part would undoubtedly be *L'Anima del Filosofo* (Haydn). In the final scene, to depict Hades (?) the entire stage was given over to a shallow pool, at the sides of which were rows of doorways exiting directly into the wings. This meant that any artist who stepped through a door onto the stage was immediately paddling in 6 inches of water. Dubbed as 'the shower scene', water continually rained down on the proceedings as well, so everyone inevitably got thoroughly wet. All choristers involved in this scene wore a brown shift of eminently washable material and were issued with rubber scuba bootees and a pair of knickers to wear under the brown shift when on stage. Only the ladies chorus were involved in the action on-stage, but to accommodate the gents' vocal contribution, there were some strange 'holes' in the pool floor and the men would stand in the Mezzanine below the stage and poke their heads out in order to sing their lines. The ridiculousness of their situation was not lost on the most irreverent of the male chorus - and on several occasions, we found a yellow plastic duck floating after they had made their final exit. The end of the opera is one of pandemonium as all on stage try, but fail, to escape a watery death. A scene of such mayhem needs choreographing with precision in order for it to work safely and successfully. Everyone had a specific cue on which to make a mad dash to exit a particular door. As you reached your open door at the side of the set, a member of the stage crew who had been positioned behind it, would slam the door in your face and you would then fall down 'dead' back into the water (face up of course). You then had to lie motionless in the water during the rendition of the final histrionic aria, until the character singing it also expired. One evening, one of the ladies, Jenny, had the misfortune to slip and fall as she sprinted through the water towards her doorway. By the time she recovered herself, winded but no bones broken, she realised that we had all reached the side of the stage and were playing dead. She also realised that she was right in the middle of the stage, exactly where leading lady Cecilia Bartoli was to die. She found herself in an unenviable Catch 22 situation. Should she stay 'dead' where she was and risk compromising the diva's tour de force aria? On the other hand, should she try to crawl out of harm's way? Neither option appeared to have any discernible merit. She (unwisely?) decided on the latter - treating the astonished audience to the sight of a 'dead' body creeping very slowly, like a large brown slug, towards the wings....

FUNNY BUSINESS

In the classic Franco Zeffirelli production of *Tosca*, several of the gents chorus were cast as church choristers, and a group of boys and young men were recruited to sing and act out the scene of high jinks and jollity, immediately prior to the sudden arrival into the Church of the hated Chief of Police, Baron Scarpia. Traditionally, six of the ladies chorus were also dressed as choirboys to sing and act in this scene. The joke amongst the female choirboys was that demotion to a 'Townswoman' in the congregation was the writing on the wall - especially if you had been playing a choirboy for 20 years or more. I was a choirboy - and fortunately for me the production itself was retired before I was. I had a fun bit of 'business' in this scene. Whilst most of the others were jumping around the pews, celebrating the fact that Napoleon's defeat meant extra church services (and more pay), I had to climb up a ladder onto the scaffold platform where the artist Cavaradossi had been painting a religious portrait. There I discovered a few strategically placed sheets of sketching paper, one of which I then had to fashion into a paper aeroplane. An enthusiastic member of the stage management team had given me a tutorial and a few handy tips on how to make an aerodynamically perfect paper dart. On the third of the three menacing chords that heralded Scarpia's arrival, I would launch my missile into the air - willing it to sail right out over the stage, maybe even making it into the orchestra pit (which it did on two occasions). Scarpia's arrival brings the jubilation to an abrupt end - and his angry outburst causes us all slink off suitably chastened. One evening the great baritone Ruggiero Raimondi was playing the role of Scarpia. He struck an impressive and formidable figure in his Chief of Police costume - tall, broad shouldered and a full head of black hair, with its distinctive white streak at the temple. Oh dear! My dart only managed a pathetic arc before coming to land gently, but squarely, on top of his head.

Even more enraged, Scarpia turned and glared at me (in character) as he shook the missile free. Blushing furiously, I have never scrambled down a ladder so fast in my whole life. Fortunately I was able to ascertain that he had indeed seen the funny side of this when I went to apologise later in the wings.

'CHOIRBOY'

Sometimes there is a long gap between entrances for the chorus in a show, and this can provide too much time for imaginations to run riot and facilitate the hatching of silly plots. In one production of *Cosi fan Tutte,* the chorus were all in 'eastern' dress - the gents in harem pants, flowing silk shirts and waistcoats, finished off with a bushy moustache and a fez, and the ladies in full navy blue silk burkhas. One evening two choristers decided to swap costumes (I will name no names...). Although the audience would have been totally unaware of their deception, it provided us all on stage with an evening of pure delight and amusement throughout - and we all decided *she* looked absolutely great with a moustache!

BURKHAS

One of the most popular and regularly performed operas at Covent Garden is Puccini's *La Bohême*. The beautiful and traditionally staged John Copley production has been in the repertoire for thirty-five years and for twenty-five of these I have assumed the character of 'Fleur' the flower seller in the Act 2 Christmas Market scene, lugging around an extraordinarily heavy wooden tray filled with increasingly tatty silk flowers. I sell my posies to particular colleagues at certain times and in specific places on the set as laid out in the production book - but over a period of time, with new recruits and an ever changing troupe of children being absorbed into the production, the 'business' aspect had become rather fluid. I occasionally would find myself in solitary splendour - no one around with whom to react or attempt to sell my merchandise. Then one day I had a brilliant idea. I bought a bag of Jelly Babies, secreted them amongst my floral stock and offered one as 'change' when someone bought a small bunch of my flowers. It worked! Word swiftly went round and from Billy-No-Mates, I became the Pied Piper of Hamelin, with colleagues - and particularly the children on set - very keen to sample my wares. Over the years it has become quite an institution and we get through at least two large bags every show. When I go into my local shop to buy up his entire stock of Jelly Babies, the proprietor, Ali, always smiles at me knowingly: "Aha! You are going to the opera again," he says.

* * *

In Puccini's *Turandot*, the Ice Princess does not sing until about three-quarters of the way through the first act, but she appears on stage quite near the beginning of the show, to silently condemn to death several unsuccessful suitors. In our acclaimed production, directed by Romanian-born Andrei Serban, Turandot arrives on the scene standing on a litter carried on the shoulders of four hefty actors. At least that was the direction given to Dame Gwyneth Jones, the first soprano to sing the role in this production. It must have taken a lot of courage to stand immobile with folded arms on a wobbly platform, whilst being paraded around the stage by four strange men. She probably would have preferred to sit quietly in her dressing room, psyching herself up for what is undoubtedly the Everest of Italian operatic roles, but she did this uncomplainingly in every performance. Subsequent Turandots were not uniformly as gung-ho as Dame G - and gradually the litter was adapted to suit. First, a pole to *lean* against was added, followed by a carved chair to *sit* in. After that, as the Ice Princesses became a little more, shall we say, *substantial*, it was carried by six hefty actors. Then there was the addition of two shoulder height 'legs' with castors on, camouflaged by the middle actor on each side. Eventually the ingenuity of the props team was severely tested - a Turandot of vast proportions arrived, in the form of the American soprano Sharon Sweet. Four more legs with castors supplemented the specially strengthened platform - and as this Turandot trundled slowly onto the stage, one of the chorus gents was heard to remark laconically: "Something from the Sweet Trolley, anyone?"

* * *

One production of Verdi's *Macbeth* had the set consisting of a giant series of steps which we all had to clamber up, down and over in the various scenes. The famous Banquet Scene had Lady Macbeth slowly making her entrance down the staircase while we all stood on the various levels, bowing in homage as she passed. The great Russian soprano Ghena Dimitrova was playing the role of Lady Macbeth and, with her statuesque figure and formidable voice she gave a magnificent portrayal of this terrifying character. The first orchestral stage rehearsal had us all in our own clothes whilst last minute alterations were made to costumes. Ms Dimitrova appeared at the top of the steps and proceeded to walk down regally, briefly acknowledging her 'subjects' and carefully timing her descent so that her first sung line coincided exactly with the moment she reached the front of the stage. Despite her plain brown jumper and skirt and flat sensible shoes, she cut a commanding figure as she progressed through the serried ranks of chorus Courtiers. We then became aware of the fact that she was calmly chewing some gum as she negotiated the steps. Our rapt fascination of this rather unusual occurrence rapidly turned to consternation as she neared the front of the stage - and her vocal cue. How on earth would she dispose of it? *Surely* she could not spit it into the orchestra pit! Or - horror of horrors (from a singer's point of view) - *SWALLOW it*? We held our breath... With a heartbeat to go, she deftly removed the gum from her mouth, stuck it firmly behind her right ear and seamlessly launched her opening salvo...

* * *

An odd fact about the rarely performed Rossini opera, *William Tell*, is that its most famous tune - universally known as the theme from the television cowboy series *The Lone Ranger* - only features in the overture. The catchy "da da dum, da da dum, da da dum dum dum" is not repeated at any time throughout the whole of what turns out to be a very long opera (four and a half hours). The Opera House had secured the services of American tenor Chris Merritt to sing the fiendishly high tenor role, and there was a great deal of excitement generated throughout the operatic media in anticipation of this long awaited gem. The morning of the General rehearsal found everyone assembled on stage during the overture, as it would have been the first time the cast had heard the ROH orchestra play this through - and the curtain would go up as soon as the overture finished. There is a haunting oboe solo immediately before the trumpet fanfare that heralds the celebrated tune. At this point, a door into the 'prop dock' at the side of the stage was flung open and two of the stage crew, dressed up as the Lone Ranger and his sidekick Tonto, burst out into the wings and proceeded to gallop with great gusto around the stage as the orchestra unwittingly launched into their 'theme tune'. Disappearing almost as suddenly as they had arrived, they left the whole cast with huge grins on their faces as the curtain rose. Fortunately the opening scene was one of celebration!

HAIR RAISING

A wig can play a major part in the transformation into a particular character, but an unbecoming one may also trigger the maximum amount of unhappiness and embarrassment. Ron Freeman was the Wig Master at the ROH when I joined the company. He was a larger-than-life character and a very nice man - but even today a wig perceived to be hideous is still known as a 'Ron's Revenge'. Sometimes it can be quite difficult to come to terms with wearing a wig of a particular style or period. What was once the height of fashion can appear to be deeply unflattering and so far removed from modern taste that you just hate being seen in it. Unfortunately, we simply have to grit our teeth and get on with it. Some wigs are incredibly elaborate:

MASKARADE

Others, no more than a 'Bad Hair Day':

ELEKTRA    *CARMEN*

'Period' hairstyles can be most effective:

'SCHOOLGIRLS' IN *TALES OF HOFFMANN*

My heaviest, most uncompromising wig was the Geisha wig for *Madama Butterfly*. The hair used for this was over four feet in length and it warranted a personal dressing station of its own in the dressing room. Ladies from the wig department were on hand to manoeuvre them into place and anchor with many heavy duty hairpins, as the final stage in the complicated dressing process.

BUTTERFLY'S FRIEND 'MISS PEONY'

149

At the other end of the scale were the 'baldies':

GLUM 'BALDIES' GLENYS AND BARBARA SHELLEY

We hated it when these appeared on a Costume Breakdown, as they had to be stuck to the forehead, temples and nape of the neck with spirit gum, which always proved awkward and difficult to remove at the end of the evening.

In one production of *Nabucco*, the director wanted us to prepare for exile into slavery by having our hair cut off. Some of us were fitted with wigs that had a few extra tresses sewn in. During the action, our on-stage partner had to wield large scissors and actually hack these chunks of hair off, throwing them on to the floor with a theatrical flourish. This was quite nerve-wracking for the 'hairdresser' as the extra tufts had to be precisely located in order not to destroy the wig for future use.

**KATH WILDER WIELDS
THE SCISSORS**

Although it is a long opera, the Ladies Chorus only appear briefly in Wagner's *Götterdämmerung*. One production had everybody dressed like Lyons Corner House 'Nippies' (simple black dress, small white apron and an identical black bobbed hairstyle).

ROH 'NIPPIES'

Probably due to financial constraints, the wigs provided were synthetic, pre-styled, elasticised 'pull on' jobs. Dressed so, we had to walk in single file onto the rear of the stage behind a row of canteen type tables and stand in a row with our backs to the audience. At a certain musical cue we all had to drop suddenly to the floor, then stand up to face the audience about thirty seconds later on our next musical cue. One memorable evening, Elizabeth Sikora's wig managed to fall off completely as she collapsed to the floor. Frantically she struggled to put it back on whilst we were crouched in the small space between table and backcloth. A desperately short few bars later we all stood up to find poor Elizabeth, in her scramble, had managed to put her wig on back to front - she was now peering through a jaw length fringe! Despite our tangible amusement (shoulders heaving and tears rolling down our cheeks), it probably went unnoticed by the audience - as at that precise moment, the soprano playing the lead role of Brünhilde appeared on one side of the stage, climbed onto the nearest table and walked slowly across all the table tops to the other side. *She* was wearing a large brown paper bag over her head...

COUGHS AND SPITS

When I joined the Royal Opera, the company employed several House Principals who undertook many of the secondary roles in productions, and a major perk for a chorister was the opportunity to undertake and sing the even smaller roles in an opera. Universally known as "coughs and spits", they vary in importance and are sometimes only a couple of bars long. Two or three times a season, auditions were held for all the forthcoming 'Small Parts and Covers' that were to be offered to choristers. The audition usually consisted of the hopeful candidate singing a short extract from the role on offer - but this would occasionally turn farcical when the entire role comprised only a few notes and the major portion of the appropriate vocal section of the chorus turned up to battle it out. In addition to the chance to earn some extra cash (featured roles often required extra rehearsals and attracted a performance fee as well), the kudos gained from doing these roles was a great incentive. It was a great boost for one's ego to land an auditioned role, as it was then customary for the performer to have their photograph and 'biog' in the official programme. Unfortunately, the advent of the admirable ROH Young Artists' Programme has now negated the need for House Principals. Quite understandably, the small parts are now being offered primarily to these 'up and coming' young singers - with the result that opportunities for choristers to stretch their capabilities have virtually dried up. So I look back on the many roles I was fortunate to enjoy with enormous satisfaction and pleasure. These ranged from comparatively high profile 'named' characters - Ida (*Die Fledermaus*); Olga (*The Merry Widow*); Modestina (*Viaggio a Reims*) and Gabriella (*La Rondine*), as well as Milliner (*Der Rosenkavalier*); Chief Hen (*Cunning Little Vixen*) and Newspaper Seller (*Death in Venice*). Smaller roles described the character in question, often when there were more than one appearing, for example: 'Bridesmaid' (*Marriage of Figaro* and *Der Freischutz*); 'Lady in

Waiting' (*Les Huguenots*); 'Page' (*Lohengrin*) and 'Apparition' (*Macbeth*). Sometimes I was only credited in the programme as 'Solo Voice' (*Prince Igor* and *Il Seraglio*), but nevertheless each performance often generated as much nervous excitement in me as if I had been doing the lead role.

MODESTINA
(IL VIAGGIO A REIMS)

'NEWSPAPER SELLER'
(DEATH IN VENICE)

THE MILLINER in *DER ROSENKAVALIER*

Some roles demanded a lot of tricky 'business' and important interaction with the principal singers - one of these being the Milliner in the 'Levée' scene in Act 1 Scene 2 of *Der Rosenkavalier*. The Marschallin is in her boudoir giving audience to various sellers and plaintiffs, the process of which is presided over by the Major Domo. Laden with four large hat boxes, the Milliner joins the queue of hopeful vendors and sings a few lines extolling the virtues of her designer hats. As she reaches the front of the queue she has to hand over her visiting card to the Major Domo, before being ushered over to the Marschallin who is sitting centre stage having her hair styled by her on-stage hairdresser (actually the ROH Wig Master in a very fetching costume). Once she has the Marschallin's attention, the Milliner then has to kneel down and very quickly retrieve hats from the boxes, return the rejected ones, until - hooray! - a particular hat gains approval and she makes a sale. Then she has to gather up all the boxes, accept the proffered payment from the Major Domo and make a swift exit to one side. This all has to be accomplished within a very strict musical time limit. It was quite nerve-wracking because one small slip would upset the whole routine. In order to help me achieve a trouble-free performance, a member of the Stage Management would attend to me in the wings just before my entrance onto the stage. Before picking up the hat box ribbons in each hand in strict order, I needed to double-check that the correct hat rested a particular way round in the correct box, with the lids eased slightly so I could open the boxes swiftly. Then at the last minute, the ASM would slip my visiting card between the thumb and forefinger of my left hand, so I could easily present this with my upstage hand to the Major Domo. One evening, the Major Domo took the card from my outstretched hand, glanced at it as usual and then, with a big grin on his face, led me over to Dame Felicity Lott who was playing the Marschallin. This time, he handed *her* the card, which she also looked at. Her customary (scripted) look of boredom (until the final hat takes her fancy) immediately turned to one of interest and amusement. This was the easiest sale I had ever made! Later, I retrieved the card and found that someone from Stage Management had written on it, in beautiful script:

"PRESENTING
MISS GLENYS GROVES
AND HER AMAZING HAT BOX JUGGLING
TRICK"

I think my most embarrassing event occurred one evening in *La Bohême*. For many years I played the role of the Innkeeper's Wife at the start of Act 3. Although this was a non-singing part, it was quite important in the scheme of things as Mimi addresses this character directly, entreating her to ask Marcello to come out of the tavern. The costume I wore for John Copley's traditional production at the ROH was without doubt the heaviest and most cumbersome outfit I had ever encountered. The underskirt was incredibly full, made of double thickness heavyweight cotton lining material. Over this, I wore a long sleeved dress with a very full gathered skirt, fashioned from what can best be described as thick tweed upholstery material, trimmed with heavy woollen fringing. A heavy moleskin apron, a voluminous lace trimmed bonnet with 'Deputy Dawg' ear flaps and thick hand-knitted fingerless gloves completed this fetching ensemble. The sheer quantity of fabric used to fashion these garments made me resemble Beatrix Potter's Mrs Tiggywinkle and it certainly had the desired effect. The costume was so cumbersome I was forced to walk just like Mrs Tiggywinkle at all times. However, it was a cameo part I thoroughly enjoyed playing as there was such a lot of business to do and it was fun to be involved and interact with principal characters. Let me set the scene:

It is in the early hours of a bitterly cold winter's morning and snow is falling. The Innkeeper's Wife (me) is trying to send home the last stragglers from the bar. I manage to evict one drunken patron, shut the pub door and then proceed to sweep the snow off the veranda to clear the pathway. A customs guard comes over to the balustrade and asks for some soup. I then go back into the tavern, stow my broom behind the door and pick up two bowls of steaming hot soup, conveniently placed by a member of the Stage Management. (As the guard and his companion have to look as though they are about to eat the soup, they have negotiated with the Stage Management that the soup is always both tasty and hot). A customer inside (one of the actors) opens and closes the pub door behind me, as I am carrying a bowl in each hand. On handing the soup to the guard, I check over his shoulder to let him know when Mimi, who has entered the scene, is at a certain position behind him so he can turn at the right time to acknowledge her. I then turn away from the guard, see a galvanised bucket containing several empty wine bottles in the corner of the veranda and waddle over to pick up the bucket. Next, I negotiate the three steps down onto the floor of the stage and then proceed to the centre of the scene where a crate for empties has been set. Whilst putting the bottles (as silently as possible) into this crate I am approached by Mimi - who is coughing and is obviously very unwell. She asks if I know of Marcello and grasps my arm as she emphasises that I am to tell him that Mimi is outside and urgently needs to speak with him. I then pat her hand reassuringly and, bucket in hand, return up the steps (terrifically hampered by my huge skirt) and back into the tavern to signal to the waiting Marcello that his presence is required on stage. (I usually tell him it is a Parking Warden, the Tax Man, or Santa Claus - but that often falls flat when the chap playing Marcello does not speak much English).

Anyway, all usually goes well with my little scena - but this particular evening, the bucket with the empties had been set much closer to the doorway than usual - and unfortunately I hadn't noticed this during my initial snow clearing. I emerged from the bar, a brimming bowl of hot soup in each hand. As I swept round to face Brian the guard, the thick woolly fringing on my skirt entangled itself with the handle fixing of the galvanised bucket, which promptly upended itself. With a horrible clatter, three empty wine bottles rolled off the veranda and crashed down onto the stage floor. They then proceeded to roll perilously towards the orchestra pit, coming to rest by the empty crates. I was mortified! Mimi was staggering towards Brian, coughing pitifully. I thrust the soup into his outstretched hands and tried, unsuccessfully to extricate the bucket from my fringing, but as I turned, the stupid thing just swung tantalisingly out of reach. I then realised that if I did not get a move on I would miss my 'Mimi moment', and the poor woman would have no one to enquire as to Marcello's whereabouts. I struggled down the steps (Oh the noise!!) and gathering up scattered wine bottles, I just about reached the crates as Mimi began to address me: "Oh, buona Donna..." Naturally, she was completely immersed in her character and I certainly did not want to bring any further attention to my plight, so I just silently mouthed: "Sorry", gently patted her hand and clanked off to summon Marcello.

Needless to say, at *every* subsequent performance I made sure that I was down on stage before curtain-up to Act 3 to check the position of my props.

* * *

The opera in which I had the most fun during the rehearsal period and the subsequent performances was definitely Janacek's *The Cunning Little Vixen*. The majority of the cast played animals and birds and the costumes and sets were quite fantastic. I landed the role of Chief Hen, which meant I was the shop steward leader of a group of comical chickens who busied themselves laying eggs in a Heath Robinson style automated chicken coop. All the choristers playing hens and the various woodland creatures spent some most enjoyable rehearsal time with the wonderful choreographer Stuart Hopps, perfecting the animal movements necessary to do justice to our costumes and characters. The hens wore huge stuffed body suits to give us an overly plump chicken shape, under a white double-breasted overall. A white chef's hat, beak, white rubber gloves and pink wellingtons completed the transformation. Our march on stage, doing our exaggerated chicken movements, elicited a round of applause every show. My main task as leader is to appear to be in charge - after all, I had the shop steward's whistle hanging on a cord around my neck. Whilst my hen colleagues work busily on the production line, laying and boxing their eggs, I file my nails (I had red nail polish painted on my 'Marigolds' and an oversize emery board in my breast pocket): "Trrrrrppp!", and flirt with the Cockerel (another wonderful costume). The Vixen then approaches the chickens, briefly gaining their confidence, before embarking on a killing spree. Chickens run in all directions but are despatched swiftly and efficiently by the murderous Vixen. As her final target, I launch into my precisely choreographed headless chicken act. I am chased all over the set, running, jumping (not easy when you are wearing a 16 tog duvet), screeching: "Kokodak! Kokodak!" until I am at last garrotted - and with a final "Squawk" I die heroically - centre stage. I then lie there, trying not to pant after all that exertion (I am dead, after all), for several more minutes, hoping desperately that I have landed in the correct place as the curtain will come sweeping in at the end of the scene and I certainly don't want to be downstage of it when it does....

A 'DEAD' CHICKEN - CENTRE STAGE

During my time at the Royal Opera, we performed this opera in three different seasons and I was fortunate to play the Chief Hen on each occasion. The second time it was produced it was sung in Czech, the original language. Whilst everyone else had to re-learn the words, I was delighted to find that "Trrrrrppp!" and "Kokodak!" were exactly the same in Czech.

Undoubtedly the most prestigious role I was fortunate to land was that of Ida in *Die Fledermaus*. It is a great character and she appears throughout the whole show, with loads of interaction with the principal artists. *Die Fledermaus* is a frothy, fun show and in the Act 3 party scene it is traditional for guest artists to appear and perform a cabaret entertainment. In our production, two principal soloists from the Royal Ballet undertook this. However, we had a scheduled performance one New Year's Eve and to our amazement, the rumour went round that Dame Joan Sutherland had elected to take the opportunity of making her farewell performance at the Royal Opera House. Dame Joan's husband, Richard Bonynge, was conducting the show - and then we heard that he and Dame Joan had managed to persuade none other than Marilyn Horne and Luciano Pavarotti, both long-time friends, to join her in a fifteen minute cabaret spot! What an amazing surprise and treat for cast and audience alike. A live television broadcast and a video recording were scheduled. As Ida was a minor principal role, I occupied a dressing room on the Principal Floor for this show (much kudos). When I arrived for the rehearsal on the morning of 31st December, the Stage Manager met me at the Stage Door. He was very apologetic, but hoped I would understand - with the extra VIP Principals, the dressing room situation had become somewhat critical - would I mind vacating 'my' dressing room this one evening, to accommodate Dame Joan? Of course I agreed and went immediately to the Principal Floor to clear away my personal bits and pieces and take them back down to join the girls in the Ladies Chorus dressing room. Before I could complete this task however, the door opened and in walked Dame Joan herself. She immediately assessed the situation and said, very firmly, in her distinctive Australian drawl: "Oh no, don't you *dare* move out for me - I'll go in with Marilyn next door - we have such a lot of catching up to do!!" Despite protestations from both the Stage Manager and me she was most insistent - and judging from the peals of laughter that emanated from the neighbouring room throughout the evening, their reminiscences were all very jolly. So that is how I spent one of the most memorable evenings of my whole career - in a solo dressing room with maestro Pavarotti on one side and Dame Joan Sutherland and Marilyn Horne (sharing!) on the other. Could it ever get any better for a chorister???

IDA - *DIE FLEDERMAUS*

CONTROVERSY

In recent years, opera productions have courted controversy as directors struggle to find something innovative that could possibly appeal to younger audiences. Unfortunately, this can often have the effect of alienating the core 'traditionalists' and there would appear to be a very fine line between 'edgy' and 'ridiculous'. The audiences, too, are nowadays certainly not shy when it comes to expressing displeasure at a production perceived to be pushing the boundaries a little too far. Quite often, during the rehearsal period, we would have an inkling as to how an audience would react to certain scenes which were perhaps bordering on the realms of dubious taste. One example immediately springs to mind. At the end of *Les Huguenots*, the Ladies chorus were dressed as modern day nuns (belted grey raincoats and black wimples). We came onto the stage pushing prams - when we were promptly machine gunned down by the Gents chorus, dressed as soldiers...

However, I shall never forget the first time concerted booing greeted the curtain call on the first night of a new production. This was *Fidelio* - and a traditional portrayal of brave and unconquerable wifely devotion it certainly was not. The director had some pretty wacky ideas throughout the show and these culminated during the final glorious chorus, when Leonora liberates her beloved husband from incarceration in prison. Three stilt walkers, terrifyingly dressed as demons with huge wings stalked about amongst the singers - who were all standing motionless; uniformly clad in cream woollen shifts and cream pointy hats. On hearing the final orchestral chords, everyone had to raise their arms above their heads, palms pressed together as if in prayer, as the curtain slowly descended.   We remained in this position as the curtain lifted for a first 'picture call'.   There were a few seconds of stunned silence before it seemed that all hell had been let loose - a barrage of boos and catcalls came from all areas of the auditorium.   The conductor, Sir Colin Davis, seemed visibly shocked - after all, the orchestra had played magnificently and there was certainly an 'A list' raft of soloists.   Quite shaken by the vehemence of the reaction we had to stand there, arms aloft, until mercifully the curtain came down again.   There have been (*far too many*) other occasions since this when members of the audience have vociferously expressed their disapproval of a show - but the first time was an unforgettable and quite upsetting experience.

* * *

One highly controversial production needed no exaggeration in order to shock - the scandalous story with its elements of wantonness, seduction, murder, black magic and evil was sufficiently horrific enough in itself. Prokofiev's *Fiery Angel* ends with an entire convent of nuns being possessed by demons.   A troupe of Russian gymnasts from the Kirov Opera in St Petersburg was engaged to play the demons.   Their 'costume' comprised nothing more than a grey posing-pouch and head to toe grey body make-up.   They spent the whole show menacingly hanging from and climbing up and down wall bars positioned around the set, until the very last shocking scene when they leave their perches and take possession of the nuns - tearing their habits off in an orgiastic frenzy. We were informed that nuns in the period in which the opera was set would have had their hair shaved off and for realism we were all required to wear 'baldies' (a cap of thin rubber covering our hair), so when our wimples were pulled off, our bald heads would be exposed.   Some of the more uninhibited actresses and extra choristers even succumbed to financial persuasion to end up topless as the curtain fell. The rehearsal period was very interesting as naturally the young Russian gymnasts were very 'fit' in all senses of the word. Fortunately, the language barrier proved no obstacle as far as socialising with the unmarried chorus ladies was concerned. As for me - I recall travelling in for a show one evening and looking round at my fellow passengers on the Piccadilly Line. I thought: "If these people only knew that in a couple of hours I would be on a West End stage in front of a couple of thousand people, dressed as a nun, with my head shoved into a giant condom, having my clothes ripped off by near naked Russian gymnasts......."

CHILDREN AND ANIMALS

"Never work with children and animals" is an old theatrical saying - and this must surely strike fear in the heart of any director invited to put on a production of *Madama Butterfly*. No matter how traditional or wacky the concept, you cannot get away from the fact that towards the end of Act 2, Cio Cio San brings her young son onto the stage - to great dramatic effect. The youngster (whose name - rather prophetically - translates as "Trouble" in some editions of the score) is the result of Butterfly's brief liaison with Captain Pinkerton and is the lynchpin for the tragic ending of the story. He is supposed to be about two and a half years old, but of course it is highly impractical to have such a young toddler appearing on a professional stage. The Opera House gets round the problem by engaging two or three children about five years old but 'small for their age' - who appear in rotation and without much rehearsal. One evening, it was the first understudy's turn to go on - a delightful little blonde child, with more than a hint of cherub about him. He received his instructions: "Now, you go onto the stage with the very nice lady. You kneel down in front of the very nice lady. You look up at the very nice lady. And you *do not move*! Got that?" He met each pronouncement with a very solemn nod of his bouncing blonde curls. The time for him to make his Royal Opera début arrived and, to give him his due, he acted perfectly - he walked on stage hand in hand with the very nice lady. He knelt down in front of the very nice lady. He gazed up adoringly at the very nice lady. He *did not move*. That is, until Butterfly launched into her 'Suicide Aria' - at which point he clamped both hands firmly over his ears and remained, transfixed, until the end of the scene.

We were doing a production of *Katya Kabanova* - a very bleak and harrowing opera by Janacek. The director was the well known and highly respected theatre director, Sir Trevor Nunn. He was determined that the production should be as true to life as possible so the dark and complex nuances of the relationships would be highlighted. The story centres on Katya, a young bride, whose husband departs the village on a protracted business trip not long after their wedding - leaving her at the mercy of the mother-in-law from hell and a predatory and very persuasive ex-boyfriend. (A certain recipe for an operatic tragedy of monumental proportions, if ever there was one!) In order to bring home the point that the young bridegroom was leaving for a lengthy trip, Sir Trevor decided that he should travel away from home by horse and cart, not on foot. The Company hired a real animal to pull the cart across the stage following the young man's farewell to his family. Every performance, the horsebox would arrive in Floral Street a couple of hours before the show and the horse would be led through the side entrance to the stage (the Scenery Dock) and tethered at the rear of the stage, waiting for his big moment. Of course, the novelty of having a live horse backstage in the theatre was not lost on the many animal lovers in the cast and crew, and most managed to find their way to the dressing rooms etc. via the backstage area in order to say "hello" and proffer a titbit or two. Over the weeks of the rehearsal and performance period, the horse got visibly fatter and fatter - with dozens of people feeding him carrots, apples and polo mints. One evening, already harnessed into the cart, he was patiently waiting in the wings for his cue to go on stage. I would like to explain here that *every* entrance onto the stage at the Royal Opera House *has* to follow a cued instruction delivered by one of the several Assistant Stage Managers (ASMs) working in the wings, who are relaying the cues written into the musical score during production rehearsals. Everyone - Pavarotti, the chorus or a horse - will have a "Stand By" cue, before being issued with a "Go" at the correct musical moment, and it is *just not done* to go onto the stage without this official say-so. The tenor was singing a fond farewell to his grandmother, during which the horse and cart would come onto the stage. At the climax of his aria, he was to throw his luggage onto the back of the cart, jump on after it and be transported into the great wide world. A few bars before the tenor's high note, the ASM gave: "Stand By, horse", then at the appropriate moment: "Horse - GO!" The horse must have thought: "What a good idea - haven't 'been' since I got here this afternoon."   And so, to the combined horror and amusement of those waiting in the wings behind him - he *did*!! After a short delay, during which time the poor tenor had finished his high note and was staring into the wings with rising panic - where was his transport? Should he wait and risk being stranded on stage with egg on his face? Should he pick up his carpetbag and walk off?   Should he just run off?   However, the horse, consummate professional that he was, realised he had missed his cue - so he took off like a greyhound out of the trap. At a brisk trot, he lumbered across the stage, necessitating the 'aged' grandmother to leap nimbly out of his way - and a mightily relieved tenor sprang heroically onto the cart and swiftly disappeared into the opposite wing. I would like to say that they caught up with him half way down Bow Street but that *would* be a slight exaggeration.   However, I do have it on good authority that one of the stagehands detailed to clear up the mess, reported a singularly good crop of rhubarb the following spring.

* * *

Another equine 'star' of the opera scene was Louis, a magnificent black stallion.   Francesca Zambello, the director of a new production of *Carmen* decided it would be a great idea if the matador, Escamillo, made a grand entrance by riding into the Act 2 tavern set. He would then sing the famous Toreador Song on horseback. Unfortunately, the baritone playing Escamillo had not ridden before, so he was scheduled several riding lessons during the rehearsal period. When it came to the shows, it certainly proved to be a 'coup de theatre' - both audience and cast gasped and applauded the stunning spectacle as Louis and Escamillo made their show-stopping entrance. After a couple of shows, however, Louis became bored with standing still in the centre of the stage whilst Escamillo sang his rather long aria, so he decided to turn round and then wander off to investigate what was happening towards the back of the set. Poor Escamillo, still a very novice rider, was unable to contend with both singing the aria *and* controlling his wayward mount, so he ended up twisted in the saddle, his back to the audience, trying desperately to face front whilst continuing to sing a difficult aria.

In the same production, Francesca originally wanted dogs and chickens wandering loose around the village square to give the scene authenticity. Management firmly vetoed the dogs, but several chickens, with their 'handlers' dressed to blend in with the chorus, appeared in the opening scenes. It was then decided to use them in the Act 3 Smugglers scene, so as well as gypsy smugglers hauling contraband over the mountain pass, Pollyanna the donkey was led across the stage and the chickens and their handlers (now dressed as gypsies) joined the chorus as they set up camp on the mountainside. My partner in this scene was a tenor in the extra chorus - a lovely Welsh farmer's son. As per rehearsal, we met on stage at our appointed place and, along with the rest of the choristers, settled down under blankets to 'sleep' whilst Carmen and her two gypsy friends, Frasquita and Mercedes, told fortunes using a pack of cards (the 'Card Trio'). After the two girls' lively interpretation of their futures, it was Carmen's turn to discover her fate. The music takes a sudden serious and melancholic turn - Carmen's cards only signify death. In the dramatic pauses between Carmen's gloomy pronouncements, there comes the unmistakable sound of a chicken...

"Oooh!" whispers Gareth in his delightful Welsh lilt, "That's the sound they make when they are laying eggs!"

Sure enough, after the show we find the chicken handlers are at the Stage Door doing a roaring trade in freshly laid eggs.

OUTREACH

In order to try and dispel the 'elitist' tag attached to opera and to reach out to a wider audience, the Opera House started to broadcast specific productions of both opera and ballet live onto giant cinema-type screens erected in public places across the country. Audiences can attend free of charge, come rain or shine. The erection of one of these screens in the Covent Garden Piazza gave rise to a decision that before the show, the Chorus Master at that time, Terry Edwards, would teach the assembled crowds a chorus from a section of the opera about to be broadcast, joined by a quartet of choristers to sing the solos in the prepared extract. I was asked to do several of these 'Singalongs' and it was such a thrill to step out onto the stage temporarily erected in front of the Big Screen and see a sea of thousands of happy faces anticipating an evening of great opera. After the show, the principal artists would come out onto the Piazza stage to receive even more ecstatic applause from an occasionally very damp audience. Eventually the Piazza screenings became so popular that they had to be suspended, due to Health and Safety concerns from Westminster Council - but the Big Screen was then moved to Trafalgar Square, where thousands more opera and ballet lovers are now able to enjoy world class performances free of charge.

At the other end of the Covent Garden Piazza is St Paul's Church ('The Actors' Church'). It has a huge portico designed by Inigo Jones, and it was against this impressive backdrop that one summer the Royal Opera Chorus gave three open-air concert performances of the Lerner and Loewe musical *My Fair Lady*. It was a complete change from our usual operatic fare and I was delighted to return to my 'West End Wendy' roots by singing the role of Eliza Doolittle in one of the performances. We garnered huge audiences from tourists and locals alike and I think we all enjoyed letting our hair down.

Apparently, the Opera House had been a popular venue for 'Tea Dances' during and after the war. Management decided to reinstate this tradition as part of a drive to make the building more user-friendly. Members of the orchestra formed an excellent dance band and hundreds of people regularly flocked to trip the light fantastic to foot tapping tunes. The chorus was approached to see if anyone was interested in singing some songs from the 1930's, 40's and 50's during the interval when tea and biscuits were served. Naturally, this was right up my street - and I became a regular vocalist at the ROH tea dances. Moreover, I especially enjoyed honing my ballroom dancing skills in the second half of the programme. One day it was decided that, fronted by a couple of the professional dancers from BBC's *Strictly Come Dancing*, an attempt would be made to create a record for the highest number of couples dancing at a tea dance, switching the venue to none other than Trafalgar Square. Dervla Ramsay and I were thrilled to be invited to sing with the band on this momentous occasion - a gloriously sunny summer afternoon in an absolutely packed Trafalgar Square, with happy 'regulars' and tourists all waltzing into the Guinness Book of Records.

**GLENYS AND DERVLA ENTERTAIN THE TEA DANCERS
IN TRAFALGAR SQUARE**

The ROH Education Department provides important outreach to schools and institutions and I was keen to be involved in the Schools Programme running at the time I joined the Company. This then comprised three separate workshop shows, targeted at pupils of different age groups. The most popular one was entitled 'Quarrels', aimed at 10 - 14 year olds. In this, four singers (led by two House Principals) and a pianist presented a well-structured workshop that demonstrated different ways in which disagreements are portrayed in opera. It culminated in every youngster being involved in a scratch performance of the Act 2 quarrel scene from *Eugene Onegin*, with us singing the solo roles. A more thought provoking workshop entitled 'Family Relationships' covered the 15 - 18 age group, and a fun filled 'Happy Ever After' gave many 6 -9 year olds their first taste of opera. Each session lasted three hours and, although extremely tiring for us, it was very rewarding when young people who had been fed a constant diet of pop music, realised and admitted that perhaps opera could be an enjoyable art form after all. Of course, these extramural trips had to fit in with everybody's work commitments at the House, but we managed many fun outings countrywide. On one occasion, mezzo Elizabeth Sikora and I travelled by train to Matlock Bath. John Dobson and Paul Griffiths had elected to travel by car and had agreed to pick us up from the station and take us to the upmarket girls school where we were expected for lunch before the afternoon Quarrels workshop. Elizabeth and I had enjoyed a very pleasant, uneventful rail journey and prepared to disembark from the train at Matlock Bath. The train approached the station, then slowed and came to an abrupt halt just short of the platform. We waited patiently for a few minutes, but eventually the train moved off - and continued moving through the station - where we were only able to wave gaily at the bemused John and Paul standing on the platform. Then the train picked up speed and continued for about ten minutes, before eventually coming to a complete halt, seemingly in the middle of nowhere. It was only then that Elizabeth and I realised that we were totally alone in the carriage - and there was no one in the adjoining carriages either. We were frantic! We walked through the utterly deserted train until we reached the front and the door to the driver's compartment. We knocked on the door and it was opened by a thoroughly shocked train driver, who was enjoying a lunchtime sandwich - alone, he thought. It turned out that we were in some sidings a few miles out of the town and that the guard *should* have walked through the train before disembarking at the station (which had a platform shorter than the intercity train). This all happened before the relatively recent advent of mobile phones, so the driver had to radio the station master back at Matlock, who then proceeded to direct John and Paul out into the countryside to a road closest to the field in which we were stranded. When they eventually found us, Elizabeth and I clambered down from the train (and these intercity mammoths are about seven feet above the ground). In our heels and summer dresses, we hiked across a field - only to face the ribbing of our two colleagues, who were absolutely convinced that we had been too busy chatting to notice that we had reached our destination. It was a long time before we ever lived that one down (in fact, I am not sure that we ever *really* did), but Elizabeth and I always maintain: *"There was NO platform!"*

* * *

Another sponsored aspect of Royal Opera outreach was taking an imaginatively compiled and specifically tailored programme into residential and convalescent homes and children's hospitals. This usually involved two or three singers, an orchestral player and a pianist. As well as a few popular operatic arias and excerpts, we toured a dressing up box and a Disney singalong to the children's wards, and Old Tyme Music Hall and Ivor Novello to the adult institutions. The most unusual venue, however, must be the concert we gave to inmates at HMP Ashworth Hospital - the high security psychiatric hospital in Merseyside. The security hoops we had to jump through before we even reached the site were incredibly strict - and even then it took about half an hour to be processed through into the complex. Once inside, our audience was extremely appreciative, enjoying the show immensely - but it was a very strange experience for us when we found it took even longer to get out of the Prison than it had to give the concert.

ON TOUR - AT HOME

Back in 1991, before it was torn down and rebuilt, the Company enjoyed a two week 'residency' at Wembley Arena, presenting eleven performances of Puccini's *Turandot*. Although the chorus took part in every show, the principals shared roles and performed on alternate nights, with the two main leads Turandot and Calaf playing only one or two shows each. This production has the chorus in view throughout, sitting in tiered balconies around the stage and standing to comment on the action played out on the floor below. This opera production always provided brilliant evenings for us, as we have what are arguably the best seats in the house and get to see and hear the best portrayals of these heavyweight roles in their entirety each show. At Wembley we had the benefit of hearing operatic legends such as Ghena Dimtrova, Eva Marton, Galina Savova and Grace Bumbry perform with their equally celebrated tenor counterparts - Popov, Lamberti and Dennis O'Neill. For me, the best evening was the pairing of Dame Gwyneth Jones with Franco Bonisolli. The fun started at the rehearsal in the afternoon, when Turandot advances menacingly towards Calaf and puts her hands around his throat. Franco jumped back, alarmed and obviously unhappy about this move. "But darling," Dame Gwyneth purred, "that is what the director wanted - and I did the *original* production." Clearly rattled, Franco succumbed to this perceived indignity and the rehearsal continued. However, when it came to the performance and these two protagonists slugged it out in the Three Riddles duet - singing each alternating phrase higher, longer and louder than the previous one, Franco moved in front of Gwyneth to sing his answer to her challenge. She immediately took up the gauntlet and moved in front of him to deliver her next line. He retaliated by moving in front of her.... and so, to our immense delight, it continued until Franco ended up leaping onto the prompt box right at the front of the stage to deliver his ringing top 'C'. The winner!

When, in the summer of 1997, the Opera House closed for a two and half year, £300 million 'refit', we were effectively homeless. The chorus numbers were reduced by half (an unhappy process I prefer not to dwell on) and the survivors embarked on a semi-peripatetic lifestyle, performing small-scale operas in various locations. We performed at the Aldeburgh Festival and visited the Edinburgh Festival two years running. This latter engagement proved very popular, as we were able to spend the day and late evening enjoying other folks' talent in Fringe performances - an absolute joy for an enthusiastic theatre-groupie like me. Back in London, we had been booked into the Sadlers Wells Theatre in Rosebery Avenue, which had also been undergoing a serious facelift. Unfortunately, as with most building works, the construction schedule had overrun somewhat and the theatre was definitely not finished for occupation by the time we were due to open with a run of Benjamin Britten's opera *Paul Bunyan*. The builders made a valiant effort and managed to get the auditorium and public spaces more or less fit for a paying audience, but this had a detrimental effect on the progress to complete the dressing rooms and facilities behind the curtain. In fact, for the first two stage rehearsals there were no working lavatories backstage so, in costume, we had to go out through the Stage Door (little more than a building site in itself), cross the road and use the facilities in the pub opposite. I have to say, though, that despite the deprivations of the performance infrastructure, *Paul Bunyan* (which we also took to Aldeburgh) was probably the happiest of all the shows I was involved with at the Royal Opera - we became a very close and complementary group of people, thoroughly enjoying our work, and working together. Great fun!

We moved into the Shaftesbury Theatre for six months and performed *The Marriage of Figaro, Cosi fan Tutte, The Barber of Seville* and *The Merry Widow*. Although it was a very pretty theatre 'front of house', backstage facilities left a lot to be desired. The dressing rooms were very compact and the ones allotted to the chorus were on the top (fourth) floor. So many stairs - and another theatrical tradition prohibits the use of a lift during a performance. In addition, the stage area was considerably smaller than that to which we were accustomed. The small scale Rossini and Mozart operas coped admirably with this disadvantage, but it proved quite a handicap when mounting *The Merry Widow*. For a start, we had to offer a set that lacked the almost obligatory sweeping staircase - otherwise there would have been no room whatsoever for the other Merry Widow 'must have' - dance routines! Unfortunately, most of the opera critics mentioned the missing staircase in a detrimental way - but understandably, the designer had to cut his coat according to his cloth. The other major drawback (for us) was the fact that, because it was important to use every available square inch of stage space, the set went right up to the back wall of the theatre. This meant that there was no 'crossover' behind the set - so when you arrived at stage level and you were required to enter on the other side - you had to run down a further flight of steps, cross under the stage and up yet another flight of steps before you even got to *think* about going on stage. Often we had to contend with exits from one side, with a quick re-entry on the other. It meant we had to be particularly on the ball as to which side of the stage we needed to be on - and there were several instances of 'headless chickens' in the early stages of performance.

OLGA IN *THE MERRY WIDOW*

ON TOUR - ABROAD

The Royal Opera on tour abroad was always a glamorous and exciting experience. During my association with Covent Garden I had the privilege to perform with the Company in New York, Athens, Rome, Amsterdam, Baden Baden, Savonlinna (Finland), Palermo (Sicily), Seoul (South Korea) and twice in Tokyo, Yokohama and Osaka in Japan. We were always booked into five-star hotels and there were many invitations to
 official receptions and parties. A great sense of adventure and camaraderie developed within the company and it was good fun to socialise with the principals, orchestra and stage crew, instead of disappearing to our homes at the end of the day as we usually do in the UK. There have even been several 'interdepartmental' weddings as a direct result of a ROH tour.

The first overseas trip I embarked on with the Royal Opera was as an extra chorister to Japan and Korea - a mammoth six week undertaking. We performed *Carmen, Samson and Dalilah,* and *Turandot* - three 'chorus heavy' operas, but fortunately we still had some spare time to explore the cities in which we were performing.

On the morning of a scheduled *Carmen* performance in Tokyo, we heard that lead tenor José Carreras was unwell and unable to sing that evening. At the last minute, Franco Bonisolli, the tenor who had played the role of Calaf in *Turandot* the previous evening, saved the day by offering to take on the more lyrical role of the young love-struck soldier, Don José. Many company members were concerned as to what sort of job the mature Bonisolli would make of a role he had probably not sung for a good many years, and there was a great deal of consternation and speculation in the dressing rooms before curtain-up. In the event, everyone was astounded and impressed by the fine, sensitive, musical singing and committed interpretation of the Don José character maestro Bonisolli displayed that evening - not least because he remembered and performed the role flawlessly with scant musical and production rehearsal. It just went to prove that the 'old warhorse' thoroughly deserved his reputation as an opera _star_. The most memorable moment of his performance was at the end of the Act 2 Tavern Scene. The set had a huge staircase rising from the floor of the inn to a balcony occupied by many of the chorus members. As the final chorus reached its climax before the curtain fell, Franco, a tall strikingly handsome man, on an impulse swept Agnes Baltsa, his Carmen, into his arms and literally ran up the stairs carrying her. The assembled company cheered as long and loud as the audience. When poor José Carreras returned to the show for the next performance, he was horrified when presented with the prospect of a bit of extra 'business'.

The first time I visited Japan with the Company, even Tokyo was very 'unwesternised'. There were no English directions in the shops or on the railway system. We had to learn to recognise the Japanese hieroglyphics for essentials, such as 'Exit' and 'Toilet', and every task and journey seemed to take twice as long to complete. However, when we returned twenty years later, all the signs and even a lot of advertisements had English translations, which made such a difference. Nevertheless, we still managed to be caught out - approaching the checkout at a small supermarket on the way to the theatre one afternoon, on an impulse I bought a jumbo bag of savoury snacks to share with my colleagues as we got ready for the show. I gaily handed round these delicious little fish-shaped morsels - but when I offered the bag to our charming little Japanese dresser she recoiled in horror. With a great deal of giggling and miming, she managed to explain that we were enjoying _Cat Treats_!!!

An incident that occurred during our first Far East tour has remained in the memories of all who were present and has gone down in the annals of ROH touring folklore. The hotel in which we were staying in Seoul was extremely glamorous and boasted an enormous indoor swimming pool. Of course we were all keen to take advantage of this luxurious facility and one afternoon, early on in our stay in the city, several of the ladies chorus decided to visit the pool which was already proving popular with other members of the company and orchestra. We had managed to persuade Nada, the most senior member of the chorus, to join us. Unmarried and a vicar's daughter, Nada was a great colleague, but would definitely be correctly described as 'old fashioned'. She emerged from the changing cubicle resplendent in a rubber bathing hat and a bathing suit that could well have been purchased before the war. It was a pool rule that all bathers should shower before entering the water and a row of overhead showers were placed along the side wall of the pool area specifically for this purpose. Nada positioned herself under one of the shower heads and turned the controls. She must have been rather heavy handed in this action as the water suddenly gushed out with such force that her swimsuit shot straight to the floor. It could not have happened to a more unfortunate individual - but how we all laughed (Nada included)!

* * *

Our visit to New York to take part in the Lincoln Centre Festival was definitely a wonderful experience. We went with the Royal Ballet - singing for their acclaimed production of *Daphnis et Chloé* and our new production of Hans Pfitzner's *Palestrina*. In both these shows the chorus did not act on stage, but sang from the orchestra pit. However, I did cover a small role in *Palestrina* - which means that since I took part in an understudy call on stage, I can genuinely say that I have sung solo on the stage of the Metropolitan Opera House.

* * *

In Athens we had the unique experience of performing in the open air in the Acropolis - the amphitheatre below the Parthenon. The performances did not start until after 10pm, as we had to wait until darkness fell. When we entered the stage arena on the first night of *Macbeth*, a breathtaking sight greeted us - the audience were holding thousands of lighted candles. Apparently this is a tradition - and it was really magical.

One of the extra chorus ladies, best described as a 'blonde bombshell', caused quite a stir amongst the male members of the Company. She was fully aware of her charms and enjoyed disporting herself in the briefest of bikinis around the Athens hotel swimming pool in the afternoons. Quite smitten by her, one of the (unmarried) members of the Music Staff took to lying on a sun lounger when she was at the pool - wearing dark glasses - so he could surreptitiously observe her whilst ostensibly studying a music score. We enjoyed watching him watching her - and it was with enormous amusement we saw him misjudge a shift in his position to get a better view of her antics, causing him to roll off the sun bed straight into the pool. How we laughed! I only hope the score was not on loan from the ROH Music Library.

* * *

The most unusual venue we played while on tour would be the ruined castle in Savonlinna (Finland). The castle stood on an island in the middle of a lake, reached via a causeway and a drawbridge. This drawbridge always seemed to be in the raised position - so if you were late for a rehearsal or a show you were in deep trouble. The performing area was set within the confines of the castle ruins and open to the elements. A large tarpaulin had been erected roughly over the stage and orchestra area, but the audience was not protected at all. People arrived prepared with umbrellas and were quite content to sit in the rain to watch a performance. However, the orchestra members, particularly the strings, were certainly not as laid back as the audience was. They were naturally most unwilling to play their instruments in a drizzle and on occasion halted the performance - despite the fact that *Peter Grimes* is an eminently suitable opera to be acted out in a wet, windy venue. The dressing room facilities were very basic - just a few tents pitched 'out the back'. The wardrobe department coped magnificently, despite our constant moaning about the lack of space and light - and the fact that our costumes always felt slightly damp. As for the 'facilities' - well, they were even more basic - a couple of unisex cubicles balanced on a rocky ledge and accessed via a rubble-strewn track which skirted the outside of the ruins. To top it off, there were no locks on the rickety doors - so we always visited the loo in pairs.

Most of the chorus members were accommodated on the campus of a catering college set in stunning wooded grounds about 40 minutes' drive from the town. We actually had great fun out in the wilderness - walking and running in the woods, swimming in the lake and taking advantage of the on-site sauna. We also played many board and card games and found a television channel that showed back-to-back 'Lassie' films. Every day we travelled to and from the show by coach, driven by the same lovely man. On our day off, he and his family picked us up in the coach and he drove us on a sightseeing trip around the area. We ended up having a picnic and an old-fashioned singsong on the coach on the way home.

* * *

I recall a very special evening at The Royal Concertgebouw, the iconic Concert Hall in Amsterdam. We were performing a concert version of Mozart's *Don Giovanni*, conducted by our Music Director, Antonio Pappano. Sitting on the stage amongst the Royal Opera Orchestra in this beautiful, acoustically perfect building, enjoying some superb singing and playing, was a real thrill and privilege. As the ladies chorus only sing in the first half of the opera, we were given permission to leave at the interval - but most of us were so entranced we asked if it would be in order for us to return to our seats for the second half. We were so glad we did; Sir Tom Allen was playing the lead role of the seducer Don Giovanni and he contrived to sing his 'Come to the Window' aria directly to a dear lady (of a certain age) seated just above him in the front row of the wrap-around balcony. Her obvious delight was a total joy to behold - and combined with some marvellous singing from all the other principal artists it made for an evening to remember.

A ROYAL AFFAIR

Royal Galas were always glamorous and exciting occasions and we usually remained on stage during the presentation of the 'stars' to the Royal visitors.

HRH PRINCE CHARLES ON STAGE AFTER *THE FLYING DUTCHMAN*

Prince Charles often attends the opera in a personal capacity and several choristers are convinced that he knows and remembers their names...

One day we were rehearsing on stage a scene from (I think) *Medea*. The ladies were required to lie down on the stage, right at the front edge, virtually hanging over the Orchestra Pit and pretend to 'swim' (Don't ask.) I was on the outside edge of the stage and suddenly I became aware that someone was crouching down next to me right beside the proscenium arch. I turned to see who it was - Princess Diana!!! She was on an informal visit to the House and had just come through the 'Pass Door' from the Front of House to backstage. She giggled and imitated my flailing arm movements, before disappearing into the wings. It was just my luck to be doing something ridiculous at the time of such an exciting encounter!

Towards the end of our time 'in the wilderness', during the closure of the House, the reduced Company received an invitation from His Royal Highness to tea at Sandringham. Apparently, he felt we had had a bit of a rough time of late and needed cheering up. The opera company management hired a coach to transport us to Norfolk - and it was with great excitement that orchestra and chorus members assembled outside the Shaftesbury Theatre, our temporary home, early one afternoon. However, after a couple of hours driving, it soon became obvious that our coach driver was completely lost - we were not even travelling in the direction of Norfolk. Tempers became a little frayed and the poor man had to contend with 46 back-seat drivers, all giving conflicting directions. We had been due to arrive at 5pm and had a two-hour 'slot' in the Prince's schedule. Eventually we pulled through the gates at Sandringham at about a quarter to seven in the evening. We entered the Prince's private sitting room - a surprisingly homely room - with several comfortable and well-worn sofas and a lovely grand piano. There were a couple of dogs running around and a little Jack Russell made a great fuss of me - but maybe that was because I found myself sitting next to a plate of cocktail sausages? The Prince was charming, despite our embarrassing late arrival, but he had a dinner engagement, so all too soon we had to troop back onto the coach and begin our long journey home. However, there was some unexpected excitement. Before the coach pulled away from the house a large Range Rover drove up to the side door and from it stepped the unmistakeable figure of Camilla Parker Bowles. This was, of course, at a time when speculation about this clandestine relationship was rife - so discussing this sighting kept us happily occupied all the way back to London.

A few years later, the Prince held a Reception and Dinner at Buckingham Palace to celebrate his 60th birthday. At the Prince's invitation, Renee Fleming and Rolando Villazon, together with Royal Ballet Principal Artists Mara Galeazzi and Federico Bonelli, were to perform at a pre-dinner concert in the Throne Room. Fortunately for us, Renee and Rolando decided they would like to sing the 'Brindisi' from *La Traviata* - and this requires a chorus. A ballot amongst the chorus vocal sections found twelve lucky choristers being security screened for clearance to enter Buckingham Palace. Although the concert was not until 7.30 that evening, we all had to pass through Security at around 1pm. Once inside, we were taken to a suite of rooms where we could change and then directed to the 'staff canteen' where a meal was provided after the rehearsal. We were then shown into the Throne Room, where the concert would take place. Leading from the Throne Room is the Long Gallery, immediately to the right of which is the room from which members of the Royal Family make their famous 'Balcony' appearances. Of course, the doors to the actual Balcony were firmly closed, but we did manage to peer over the windowsill and experience that very special view down The Mall. I thoroughly enjoyed calling my mother on my (rudimentary) mobile phone from the Throne Room. Camera phones had yet to be invented, but there were certainly dozens of: "You'll never guess where I am!" calls made that afternoon. After the concert, we mingled with the invited guests and the Prince and the Duchess of Cornwall made a point of chatting with everyone. When His Royal Highness came and spoke to a small group of us, he apologised that he had been unable to invite us to the dinner part of the proceedings. I said not to worry; we would probably stop at the Kensington McDonalds on the way home - and the Prince roared with laughter.

A short while later, he passed by our group again. "Enjoy your burgers!" he said.
Another evening to remember.

MAGIC MOMENTS

The occasion of a special gala concert held in honour of Placido Domingo coincided with my very last evening as a 'regular' at the ROH. This concert was recorded for BBC television and has been broadcast several times, so it is wonderful to have a video recording of what was (for me) a momentous occasion. On the wall in my music room at home I have a photograph, taken at the Abbey Road recording studios in the early 1980s, of a (very young) Placido Domingo, surrounded by half a dozen (even younger) Ambrosian ladies. On the evening of this Gala concert, I took this picture into the theatre and on an impulse went up to the great tenor's dressing room. "Look Maestro," I said, "here you are at the beginning of my career and now you are here at the end!" Very gallantly, he claimed to remember that particular recording session. He then gave me a great big hug and insisted on signing the photograph.

"TO GLENYS WITH HAPPY MEMORIES AFTER 35 YEARS -
MUCH LOVE, PLACIDO"

I have been asked many times: "What is your favourite singer, opera or experience during your career?" I think that if you have read all the preceding pages you will agree there have been so many highs over the years, I have been fortunate to have such enjoyment just doing my job, but to the previous 'Magic Moments', I would add:

a)   The first production rehearsal of Director Richard Eyre's *La Traviata*. At the end of the first party scene the chorus exit, leaving Violetta alone to sing her sparkling coloratura aria 'Sempre libera'.   Dismissed from the rehearsal to take an early coffee break, but before we could actually leave the room, the relatively unknown Angela Gheorghiu started to sing her aria.   We immediately stopped in our tracks and quickly filtered back in order to listen to this wonderful singing.   Angela had played the soubrette role of Zerlina in Mozart's *Don Giovanni* less than a year before - but this was something extraordinary.   We soon realised that here was a star in the making and this show would be really exciting.   So it proved to be.   After an ecstatic reception from both audience and critics on the first night, Alan Yentob - then head of the BBC - took the unprecedented step of clearing the schedule for the following Saturday night and broadcast the show *live* on BBC2 television . It was such a privilege to be in at the start of her glittering career.

b)   Standing on stage behind Mirella Freni in Giordano's *Fedora* when the great Placido Domingo sang 'Amor ti Vieta' - a Masterclass in vocal seduction. The earth moved for me, too!

c)   *Anything* sung by Maestro Pavarotti...

Lightning Source UK Ltd.
Milton Keynes UK
UKOW07f0352090616

275942UK00008B/31/P

9 781367 595545